*The Isaiah 54 Woman:*

*Finding the Warrior within Yourself*

Chelsea E. Hill

# THE ISAIAH 54 WOMAN:

## Finding the Warrior within Yourself

*Prologue*

Welcome to our journey!

I am so glad that you have decided to join me as we seek God together to awaken the sleeping warrior within us. I am not anyone special nor do I carry any titles, I am just a young woman, at the ripe age of twenty-four, wanting to see lives transformed not only for you, but the people assigned to you. I am honored that God has chosen me to live the life that I have lived and has allowed me to write His words to you. So let's get started.

We have all heard and aspired to be like the Proverbs 31 woman, right? Well, at least I have. I can assure you, just about every Christian woman has been to at least one bible study session or more acquiring the tools to be just like her, and when we fall short it honestly becomes a little gut wrenching. Proverbs 31 is simply entitled: *"The Wife of Noble Character."* If you are anything like me, single with no children, some of her accomplishments may seem a bit out of reach. What I have come to realize is that although, for some of us, our relationship status in our natural being is single, but in our spiritual beings, we are betrothed to our heavenly father. So this passage still does apply to us. Now that our eyes have been open, this woman's accomplishments may not be so farfetched after all; we would love to be just like her, but how? This is normally how the process of growing and applying new principles in our life goes. We come to an awesome revelation but now we have so many questions that need to be answered.

For example, we would love to be able to speak wisely and give instructions with kindness. (Proverbs 31:26) Yet sometimes, we just know without a shadow of a doubt that we are right and therefore our neck and eyes have to roll while giving an indefinite "I told you so." For the wives and mothers, you would love to have your children stand and call you blessed, or have you husband praise you (Proverbs 31:28)? Sometimes, the house doesn't get cleaned and the dishes don't get washed. Have you failed? Are you not worthy of praise? Not at all, but I am sure; you may not always feel like the blessed wife or mother that the passage describes. We would love to not have fear of the future. However, we worry about what's for dinner or how we are going to pay our bills! We spend our money on makeup and shoes, trying to contour our faces like that girls we see on YouTube, and/or strut in our heels like the model on TV to make ourselves feel beautiful or accepted. We spend days working, cooking, cleaning, and making sure that everyone else in our households, or whomever else is in our lives, are better than good, but what about you? Are you okay? Are you emotionally intact? Those questions not only apply to the natural, but to our spiritual selves too. I have lived many days where I would just want someone to ask me if I was okay. Somedays, I got what I wanted, but many days, I didn't. What happens then? Do we wallow in self-pity? No! When we find our inner strength in Him, the days that we aren't okay are okay!

The infamous Proverbs 31 passage is a prime example of the woman we want to become, but what about developing the woman we are now? This is why you've stepped out on faith and opened the cover of this book.

This book is for the single women who want to become married. This book is for the single women who may not necessarily want to become married, but to just become a better person. This book is for the wife. This book is for the hurting, and depressed. I pray that wherever you find yourself that you can become better by opening the pages of this book.

...

This book was placed on my heart by the Lord a couple of years ago, but I believe I needed to come through a few more experiences, in my own life, in order to write this book for us. I strongly believe the Lord wants to give ALL women, a life of change, hope, and strength through Him. The Lord spoke to me some months ago when I was in a place that I felt that I could not retract from, and He lead me to His words in Isaiah 54 and instructed me to teach His words to His daughters. Most of you may have read through or are familiar with the previous chapter, Isaiah 53. *"But He was pierced for our transgressions, he was crushed for our iniquities; the punishment that brought us peace was upon Him and by His stripes, we are healed." -Isaiah 53:5*. In the very next chapter is the passage that gave me purpose, strength, and healing, and truly allowed the words in Isaiah 53 to become more tangible and alive within me. It awakened my inner warrior, and I pray that it will do the same for you.

The Isaiah 54 woman is specifically designed for the woman we are right this second. Some of us may be new to this Christian walk, some of us have been on this journey more years than I have been alive, and some of us may fall right there in between. The blessing in this is that it is for every woman where they stand right now. This book regarding Isaiah 54 is to help strengthen and deliver the woman we are now, before we officially reach our VIP status also known as the proverbs 31 woman, because she is NOT unreachable.

I have come to find the best part about following Christ is that we can never know Him too much. We will never be able to figure Him out one hundred percent. I love that about Him, I would not want to follow after someone who I could not grow with or that I could figure out within just a few short years because they would not have much to offer. They would have a cap on knowledge and strength. If I could figure a god out all the way, obviously He isn't big enough!

The Isaiah 54 woman is designed to set free the little girl with hurts and who picks at emotional and mental scabs from the past. It is that same little you who has never felt beautiful who hasn't been able to see yourself as fearfully and wonderfully made. It is that same teenage you whose daddy walked out and now the adult you cannot fathom the thought of calling our God Abba Daddy because that seems like a foreign concept to you. It is the same adult you who never feels worthy enough to think that God could love you more than anything in this world. That is the girl inside of you that needs to be set free, so that you can become the woman God has called you to be! The little girls inside of you is wearing warrior armor that is just too big and heavy for her to handle until she progresses into the woman who knows what each weapon is used for.

This is the start of a glorious process. The Lord and I broke down every verse together and that's how the book will be laid out. When He first told me about this journey, I was very skeptical to share my journey with you, but I am now at a place in life where every victory and every defeat makes perfect sense. They were specifically placed in my life to encourage each of you. Each verse births a new chapter and at the end of it all, I hope you will be overwhelmed with His glory at what was conceived. It is broken down to see and experience the depth of healing, hope, deliverance, and victory.

Before entering into the passage the title simply reads "The Future Glory of Zion." I believe that through these chapters, our futures will look brighter and they will be hopeful because they will be triumphant and full of Him.

You are more than welcome to read this alone or study amongst a group of young women. I encourage you to be open and honest with yourself and our Heavenly Father as we trudge through these passages together. Be fully transparent with Him, and watch Him bring glory and hope with each word. Thank you for taking this journey with me. Let's go!

Loving you,

Chelsea Elizabeth

### *The Barren Woman*

Sing, O barren woman, you who never bore a child; burst into song, shout for joy, you who were never in labor; because more are the children of the desolate woman than of her who has a husband, says the Lord.

Isaiah 54:1

"I know he's not my husband, but he really is a good guy. Although I knew it was wrong, we slept together a few times. Then it happened... I found out I was pregnant. I was excited because I see my friends either getting married on social media or having babies. I had planned to be married first, but things just happened, but at least it is finally my turn to celebrate something, right? I had been single for a while, so when he came along I was so excited that someone wanted to date me. I had my reservations because he wasn't as Christ centered as I truly wanted, but he pursued me. That's much more than I can say about a lot of other guys now-a-days. When I found out I was pregnant, I wasn't scared, but I knew if he didn't want to stay, I would be okay with that. I mean, we weren't under a covenant of marriage, so technically he wasn't obligated to stick around if he didn't want to, but he wasn't that type of guy. I was happy. I was going to be somebody's mommy! Then after I came to the realization of this new life, the cramps started. It was the worst pain that I had ever felt in my life. The spotting became heavier than I could imagine. The clumps on the pad were very unusual. The doctor informed me to wait until the bleeding stopped and then take another test. Negative. The doctor told me it wasn't unusual to miscarry in the early stages. I felt my heart rip right out of my chest. I thought it was my turn. I thought I would have someone to truly love me. I thought it was my turn to feel the unconditional love that I have been longing for. I thought that after all this time there would be someone else to appreciate all my love that had been so readily taken advantage of all of these years.

—Camille

Not every one of us may have been where Camille has been. Perhaps your story may go a little like this:

*"Well every time I get on Facebook and Instagram someone else is engaged or getting into a relationship. I personally think I am not that bad of a person. Ok, so sometimes I have an attitude, but who doesn't? Yet and still, no one good has come along. I have dated a few guys. Some were even high hopefuls, but nothing seemed to work out in the end. I love God and I enjoy our time together but I do have a deep longing to be married and have children, but I feel that sometimes He just skips right over me and blesses someone else with the very thing that I want! I have a good job, I keep myself together, and I did I mention I love God? Men should want to date me! I feel that by the time it does happen I may be too old to bare any children or even run after them. Any day now Lord!"*

Your story may not fall in any of these two categories, but nonetheless it can be very discouraging and disappointing seeing the women around us obtaining the blessings that we so wholeheartedly desire. It can be life altering feeling your body change because life is growing on the inside of you to suddenly have your body go back to normal. It can change your emotional DNA to hear a heartbeat one day, to suddenly hear the doctor declare that the life inside of you is no longer there. It can be lonely always being the bridesmaid and feeling like you'll never be the bride. It can be gut wrenchingly depressing to know that when you leave work there's a house sitting empty waiting for you to somehow fill the void of loneliness within it, but you're married. It can be insanely frustrating to work so hard to only have someone else take that promotion. All these concepts of life are very true.

In the first scripture of our passage, the Lord speaks directly to us, the barren woman. You may be thinking, why'd she say us? I have never lost a child before or I have never even been pregnant before! Not being able to bare children or experience labor is such a heavy burden on any woman, but in this passage I believe that this concept can also pertain to our other wants and desires that we may have as women, such as marriage, education, success, friendships/relationships, and everything else in between. Admit it, we want it all and we want it now!

The women in the time of Isaiah, surely, did not have the same privileges and freedoms that we have now. They could not just get up and go to a job of their own choosing, and then go hang out with their girlfriends or date whomever they wanted. No, their obligation and their purpose was the husband that was chosen for them beforehand and their household.

Women married into families to simply bare children, at least a son, to carry on the name of that entire generation. No pressure right? Now-a-days some women don't even carry the last name of their husbands if they don't want to, and in our society that's okay. The freedoms and choices we have as the new generation of women is clearly on another level. If a woman's body, in Isaiah's time, was incapable of baring a child, she was considered of no use to the world. She could not just immerse herself with work or hobbies to somehow fill the void. The task of baring children was her identity. The concept of being a life giver was what she was told that she was made for. Can you imagine the rejection she may have felt from, not only, from her husband and their family, but from their town, and her girlfriends? The laughter and taunting from the other woman who were able to achieve the very task that this woman wanted to do must not have been an easy process to go through. In this new age, if a woman chooses not to carry a child for her husband there is nothing wrong with that.

In our generation, the taunting sadly still exists. We mainly have two extremes. We either constantly compare ourselves to one another to either make ourselves feel better, or we wallow in the fact that we don't have what SHE has. Either way it has to change. Where we place our identity has to change. Year after year, and generation after generation women have always seemed to be in competition with one another. I dream of a time where women actually lift each other up and mean it. Help one another in time of need from the goodness of their hearts not for the praises of the crowd.

Do you remember the story of Hannah in the bible? (I Samuel 1) She cried unto the Lord to give her a child. That was truly her heart's desire, and though her husband, Elkanah loved her, the desire burned deeply within her. Her husband's wife, Peninnah was giving her husband children left and right, and she constantly taunted Hannah because of it (I Samuel 1:6-7). I guess you could call that early onset pettiness. Some of us may be in that exact same area as Hannah in our lives and it may not even particularly pertain to children. We may want the degree or title, the relationship, the engagement, the marriage, then the kids, the white picket fence, and the perfect career all within our terms and conditions. Yet on our way there, we have the spirit of the sister wife where we step on other women to let them know we are better than they are. We have a *get like me type* of attitude, and it needs to stop.

The Lord instructs this woman in Isaiah, whose name we do not know, to rejoice and sing for joy right where she is in her season of life! He does not tell her to taunt and gloat. Take God's advice. He is basically telling her to praise the name of the One who can bring her heart's desire.

We find comfort in our own abilities than in Him. It can be so easy to become caught up in our own desires, thinking that they will fill voids and provide happiness. It's so easy for us now to pretend like we have it all together. We show our highlight footage on social media, and we pride ourselves in never letting others know that you can't go to bed unless you cry yourself to sleep.

You can only find true stability through Jesus, himself. How? Spend time with Him. Get to know His heart before you ask for His hand.

❖

We constantly bash gold diggers. We will turn our noses up at the thought of what a person had to do to get that new car or new purse. Honey, in all honesty on this Christian walk there are gold diggers all around, or for lack of a better term: **God diggers**. They constantly seek God to get blessings from Him. They only talk to Him to receive a blessing. They "praise" for the entertainment of man, but want to receive the blessing of GOD! They could not care less about learning His will for their lives, or get to know His heart for His people.

What do you have a habit of doing to be seen by man, but wanting to receive from God? Do you sing the loudest to be heard? Do you preach from a place of pride instead of humility? Do you serve only to put it on your Christian resume or social media? Then when your plan does not work out, or God does not move fast enough, you are quick to say "But God I serve you! Where's my prize? Where's my husband? Where's my promotion?" Our prize is Him. Our prize is His love. Our prize is eternity. I am not going to lie, sometimes I fail in this area, and it becomes a shock to my life line. Then I am forced to ask myself who am I really serving? Why am I really serving?

When you allow God to infiltrate your very being, you will be victorious in all areas of your life no matter what the circumstances are or what your relationship status may currently be. Being victorious comes with knowing that your plans may not be in the plan and that His timing is absolutely perfect despite what the earthly timeclock displays.

❖

When we first get to know someone we start by getting to know their name. That same simple life principle applies to getting to know who God is too. There are many names that describe our King, yet in the ASV translation of this specific scripture in Isaiah, they use Jehovah to describe Him. While studying other versions of this verse, I noticed most of them just say *"says the Lord"*. Yet I found it interesting that this version used Jehovah to proclaim this promise to us, the barren woman.

Jehovah simply means God or Lord, but it is also the foundation for His other titles, such as Jehovah Jireh (The Lord our Provider) or Jehovah Shalom (The Lord our Peace). If we set God to be our foundation, then our peace, our provision, our healing, and our comfort will follow thereafter just as His name describes. If someone called you by your last name and then your first name how backwards would that be? However, that is how we operate when it comes to God. We call or seek out our peace, provision, or whatever else through our own abilities before we come to Him. Then, when that does not work in our favor we come back to God. Our first name is who we are and our last name is who we belong (or identify with) or even whose blood runs in our veins. It is basically our identity. He is God first, and always, who then identifies Himself as a Provider, as Peace, and as Provision. Let Him be your foundation and everything else will come. Put your life back in order with God being your first option. Seek Him first is what the bible instructs us to do in Matthew 6:33.

Seeking Him consists of spending time with Him. It simply means to worship Him. You are able to worship Him without a band too. #Facts

Now, you may be thinking, how can I worship Him, when the very thing that I want, I do not have? That is a valid question; however it opens the door to our true desires. We do not truly desire God, when we only desire his blessings, and that is a very scary place to be.

Sometimes, what you want or need, God is telling you to wait for it. This walk will have constant periods of waiting. These waiting rooms are designed to develop you for the gifts that **GOD WANTS** for our lives. They are there to develop your faith. They are not designed to be places of fear and panic, but places of faith and praise because soon enough He will come through on your behalf (Psalms 62:1-2).

When you think of a waiting room there is automatically a negative connotation that is attached with it. Most often hospitals will come to mind with hopes of bad news. However, when you are in spiritual waiting, it is not a time of sadness or fear. There were times in my waiting seasons, where I would just waste time panicking, and God would come through every time. After a while, I begin to realize that I had to renew my thinking because it became a habit whenever God's answer was to wait. I would automatically go into panic mode. What helped during these times was remembering what God had done in past seasons, and a peace would come over me (2 Timothy 1:7).

For my single sisters, in the word, it says that being single is better than being with a partner because your focus is solely on God (I Corinthians 7:32-35). When we get the husband, the baby, the promotion, then our attention will be split between our answered prayers and the Lord. Ladies, whatever you're waiting on, this is the best time to spend with Him! The waiting room is where we learn more about Him. The waiting room is where you'll find your strength (Isaiah 30:15). Don't wallow while you wait because your attention is not where it needs to be. Instead, worship while you wait.

As we revert back to our passage the bible says, *"For the desolate woman has more children than the woman who gave children to her husband."*

The barren woman who worshipped would raise more soldiers for the kingdom than she could ever naturally bare. The woman who carries children for her husband can only do so for so long before her body gives way. She will not be able to carry children forever. Why? Our physical bodies have limitations, but or spiritual capabilities are limitless through our powerful God. The barren woman can spiritually bare children of God by showing and teaching them how to overcome the pain that she herself has endured. We cannot teach what we do not know. We cannot overcome what we have never experienced.

Your worship will look different once you have been through a couple fires, not burned to a crisp, but on fire for Him! To worship is to be obedient. The women coming behind you are attached to your obedience. These women are attached to what God has called you to do. So will you wallow or will you worship?

So this season of planting, pruning, pain, and waiting may seem like much more than we can handle, but it is not. It is preparing us. There is no expiration date on that! Our bodies can handle that as long as God gives breath to our bodies and then some!

So yes, we may want all of the perks that we see our friends and peers having, but we can rejoice because God has a people set up just for us plus so much more! Let's not lose hope because every desire that we have has to be fulfilled by Him, if they are in His will for us. He is a God who makes promises not to break them, but to bring them to fruition. So if we are helping one another we won't have time to hate one another. We can be a generation of women who truly glorify and reflect our heavenly Father.

I encourage you, instead of complaining about your planting season, pray for your harvest instead. Pray for the spiritual children and siblings that God has for you. If God has placed spiritually sisters in your pathway, pray for them often. You are not on an island going through storms alone. Other people have issues and struggles just like you. Step outside of yourself and your problems to lift up another sister in Christ. Encourage each other in the Lord.

In the bible it says that Jesus became flesh and He endured all that we have to endure, yet He did it without sinning. Jesus was our example. I personally wouldn't be able to trust the words or advice of someone who has never experienced what I have been through.

Growing up I experienced immeasurable amounts of rejection, which I carried on into my adult life. I know when those feelings of rejection arise, I can go to Jesus. The very God of our existence turned His back on Jesus as He hung there on the cross for our salvation. Jesus was the ultimate Reject! He endured. He is victorious, and if He can do it, with His grace, and strength, so can I.

Sometimes we become so caught up in our have not's that when God places people right in front of us, we miss the opportunity to pour into them. We do not go through hard times or waiting periods in life just so we can be miserable. There is always a harvest behind us. There will always be another you coming behind you seeking help for depression, miscarriages, loneliness, abandonment, rape, and rejection.

Be willing to be used by Him. When we open ourselves to His timing and His will, we encounter experiences we never would have known if we operated on our own timing.

Single ladies; don't settle because you feel like God is taking too long with your spouse. Wait for God's best, and take this time to seek Him and know Him. What a story you will have for the young woman waiting for God to bring her Adam one day. Married women, endure the hard days along with the good days through God's grace. The young married woman will need you to show her how to seek Jesus when she feels like her marriage has hit rock bottom.

There have been so many times in my life where I have also been financially barren. I mean my bank account was looking bone dry. Like, literally there is no moisture in my funds and I am just waiting on the Lord to come through for me. Yet, the people around me just making it rain all over the place! Splashing and splurging! I remember being in those times and thinking now Lord I am living for you and barely making it, and they are living in sin and have food to eat and so much more, but in that time, He brought me back to this verse. He told me to look at it this way: "Sing O financially barren woman, you who have never been rich. Burst into song you who have never acquired the wealth of the earth, because more is your heavenly wealth than those who are rich from the world." In that time, though I made myself blind to it, He was providing all of my needs according to His riches in glory! So take what you're going through and allow God to rewrite a promise just for you.

Waiting isn't always pleasant. Trust me, I understand. I am a single woman myself seeing girls that I grew up with left and right getting engaged, getting married, or starting a family of their very own. It is everything that I desire in this season, and I don't have it yet because God doesn't think that it is the right time. I honestly could not agree more with Him. My flesh is impatient and ready, but my spirit is still developing and waiting is vital. If I were to get married right now, unprepared yet willing, it would be detrimental not only for me, but for my spouse. Even though I am knowledgeable about Christ, I am still underdeveloped in certain areas of my life that would hinder the survival of my relationship. I am underdeveloped in being submissive to an earthly man. I am learning to fully be submissive and obedient to Christ first.

God does not want us to step into situations unequipped to succeed, and He does not want us to wait and worry about timing. If that were the case, why wait? He knows all that we need, and He also knows all that we desire. If our focus is on our needs, wants, and desires, we miss our opportunity to see His glory, and to experience Him in His most authentic being: uninterrupted.

Not everything happens on our timetable, and we must truly learn to be content with that concept. It is easy to always want to be in control, and losing control for Him can be a bit of a struggle. Yet, for now, come to the realization that you are the barren woman, but find what you feel you are lacking in Him. In this time: Endure. Endure for the harvest coming behind you.

Don't sulk or be embarrassed of your story, trust me, I have been there too. You go through the fire to assist the ones coming behind you to victory. Rejoice, sing, burst into song because God has hand selected you to reach others for His glory!

#NotBarrenForever

### **_The Tent_**

"Enlarge the place of your tent stretch the place of your tent curtains wide, do not hold back lengthen your cords, strengthen your stakes."

Isaiah 54:2

"I do not like for others to be all up in my business, because well...it's mine! I mean, I love to be around people sometimes, but then I feel like after a while, I will truly have to open up and let them in. I only like letting a few people get close to me because everyone just ends up failing me anyway. I go to an awesome church with awesome people, but I always decline invites outside of church because keeping people at arm's length is just comfortable for me. I have one or two close friends who know pretty much everything about me. That's all I need. The people at my church don't need to know that my parents left me at a young age and as a result I have major trust issues. Or that I was always called the "dark sister" or ugly growing up so I have self-worth issues. I would just like to keep that between me and the Lord. Yet, sometimes I feel like my past interferes with my very relationship with God. It's hard for me to trust Him, too, at times. Well, whatever, I'll figure it out on my own."

—Harmony

In 2015, I moved into my own house. My God, how freeing it is to finally be in my own place! My journey to this place was not an easy one. I have moved frequently since I was a child. Both of my parents were in the military when I was growing up so staying in one place for a long time was not an option. When my parents divorced, I did live with my mother and sisters in Columbus, GA for many years. When my mother remarried, we were on the move again.

> It was never easy to start over, yet after so many times I just became accustomed to it. After the remarriage, our home structure went from a place of peace to a place of turmoil really quickly! There was a mixture of emotional and mental abuse residing in that place with us. My mother's husband was not a very nice man. Along with him, came his two children whom I love and adore very much, but I never felt like I was a good as they were. When I lived with my mother I felt that she had turned against me and my sisters. It was like she was #TeamThem! There was a deep emotional shift within that place, but I didn't know how to

channel my emotions. I was really mean, really angry, or really sad with no in between.

My mother and I were very close before she found love again. I had seen her stay strong and take care of all four girls after her husband, my father, had left her for another woman. I had never seen her cry or breakdown over the loss of her marriage. All I knew was that she continued on and never gave up on account of me and my sisters. At the time, she was my hero! Everyone always said that my mother and I looked just alike, so that made it even easier for me to want to become just like her.

When she got remarried, it was like the woman I had admired disappeared. All the strength that I had once known just vanished. Her home became a prison and we were all trapped with her. Yet she had the key but never decided to free us.

Whenever someone walks into your house, they come carrying something, whether you know it or not. They carry a certain spirit about them and when they leave sometimes those spirits can be deposited into your space. Be careful who you surround yourself with. Be cautious of who you allow in your tent or your place of dwelling. Guard your heart and use discernment about who you chose to surround yourself with (Proverbs 4:23).

I love to spend time alone, especially now that I am on my own. Every place I have lived prior to this point has been with someone else. Now, instead of going out to escape, I stay in. As we take a look at this verse, let's consider a few questions:

A. How often do you as a person open up to others (i.e. your home, resources, your time, etc.)?

B. How often do others open up their home, resources, time, etc. for you?

In Isaiah 54:2, The Lord instructs us to enlarge the place of our tent. When I think of a tent, I think of a few things. One, being obviously the most common and practical, would be a tent that you would use for camping. The other would be a tent referring to an actual home. One of my favorite books is "The Red Tent," by Anita Diamant. It's a book about a heroine by the name of Dinah, who in the bible was Jacob's only daughter. Anita gives Dinah her own story because in the bible we only know of her name and not her life.

The Red Tent was a sacred place for the woman to retreat for menstruation, but during their time together they opened up to one another and they learned different values and customs to help their families. When the brothers of Dinah got married, the woman welcomed their spouses into their sacred place and wanted to teach them their ways and include them in their customs. Again, how often are you willing to enlarge your tent for someone else?

Our personal tents are most likely our greatest source of comfort, and sometimes we just don't want to be bothered. Whether you are like me and you're single living on your own, at times having others over just doesn't sound appealing. Maybe you are in the wife and mommy category and you feel like your tent is always in shambles. You don't even feel comfortable having others over because you don't feel like your tent is ever clean enough. Plus, at the end of the day you are just plum tired to even think about cleaning! You just want five minutes to yourself after cooking for your family and chasing down the kids, and making sure the homework is complete. Ok, so maybe after all of that you need seven minutes!

"Enlarge the place of your tent, stretch your tent curtains wide." Maybe you know of someone who is in need of somewhere to stay just for a little while. Enlarge the place of your tent. Perhaps, it has been on your heart to lead an at home bible study or small group. Stretch your tent curtains wide. When we close off our resources to the world, we miss out on the people we could have encountered. How often do you open up to others?

I think of all the people who could have closed their curtains on me when I didn't have help from my parents in my life. Where would I be if God hadn't placed me on their hearts? God can easily fix a situation in someone's life, yet He chooses to include us in His power, and that is a privilege in my book, no pun intended! Have you encountered God's power through someone else? Has he equipped someone else to help you at any stage of your life? Pray about being that blessing for someone around you.

Maybe you feel as though you may not have the resources to do the tasks that God has called you to do. Listen love, if He calls you to it, He has to provide for it. Not He may provide, but He has to. He is a God that cannot lie, so if he speaks it then He will do it (Numbers 23:19)!

Do not hold back. Some of us are like Harmony we hold back from opening up our tents because we are afraid of what people will think of the inside. Our tents can even represent our very being. We may have been scarred or bruised and it is just easier for us to retreat and spend time alone so no one will know the true you. I was in this place for a long time, and it is a place that is dark and lonely. Now, I am not saying share all your business with every person you encounter. If the lady at the check-out line asks how you are doing that particular day, just say I'm well thank you. Don't go into…well my daddy left when I was five and I just don't know how I'm going to recover! That's a little much.

Honey, God sends His people at the right time to walk with you through the hurts on this side of life. The people He places in your life have been placed there for specific reasons. One reason may be they have been where you've been and they have overcome! Now, they are in place to help you do the same. Another could be they may be carrying the very peace that you are currently in need of. Do not hold back from fellowship. It is the only thing that we can take with us to heaven.

If you have ever been camping or backpacking then you know one of the essential items to bring with you is a tent. That is where you will store your items and where you will rest. I spent a summer in Montana in 2012 for a discipleship program, and before then I had only been camping one other time, and I am not even sure if that was considered the real deal. In Montana, I learned the importance of properly setting up your tent.

When assembling your tent, it pays to follow directions. Have you ever tried to put something together by only looking at the picture on the box? When you thought you knew what was best without first reading the instructions, your configuration did not end up looking like the picture of the sample. That's what happens when you try to live this life without the Word of God. You try to mimic the lives of those around you. That's not good enough, because their instructions from God, will not be the same instructions that you might receive from God although you'll both read the same Word. Every Christian should have their own *personal* relationship with God. Just because your mama and grandmama pray for you constantly does not mean that you have a relationship with Him. God does not have grandkids. Your relationship with Him is not based off of another human. Get to know Him for yourself. Develop your relationship with Him by being obedient, not only out of obligation, but out of love. If you feel that you don't love God enough. It is ok to ask Him to help you love Him above all else.

The tools needed to configure a tent consist of the tent itself, or the covering, a hammer, cords and stakes. In order for your tent to stay properly secured you must have your stakes deeply rooted into the ground, so if there's a sudden gust of wind you won't be blown away. The cords or poles are used to assemble the shape of the tent itself. They stretch to your desired length. If you don't stretch the cords long enough then your tent will be too small and it will not be assembled correctly.

Some of you are in a place in life where you have only stretched your cords to their shortest length because it is comfortable for you. Your tent is small enough just for you and a select few, and honestly you like it that way. When your tent is small your prayer may go a little something like this: *"Lord bless me with just enough for me and mine."* Why not ask for more than enough so we can bless the people around us?! "Lengthen your cords," says the Lord. Remember, the Lord is always thinking of a harvest. He doesn't love just you. He uses us to show others His goodness!

When you have assembled the tent and pulled the poles through to their maximum length the shape of the tent starts to form. When we limit our prayers and we limit our space, who we truly can become and who we could have the potential to reach decreases. Take the limits off of GOD and take the limits off of yourself! Allow Him to stretch you to His desired length for you. That is when you start to shape up and become just like Him.

After the tent is formed, you have to make sure it stays in place so you hammer the stakes into the ground. The ground represents the word of God. This Word is one you can trust, and if we stay rooted in His word, when the winds of life blow, our tent will not be shaken or forced to be displaced to a location it was never intended to be at in the first place. You will be like the tree planted by the streams of water (Jeremiah 17:8). Strengthen your stakes! Increase your knowledge. Know who God is and know who you are in Christ Jesus, and your tent will not be moved.

Your tent can also represent your heart. That is where God wants to dwell within you most. He doesn't care if you don't have it altogether. He doesn't care if it's broken or messy. He WANTS to help you and heal you from your past hurts, and your present pain. He wasn't whipped for pleasure; His stripes heal us physically, emotionally, and mentally. (Isaiah 53:5)

Some of your tents are the inner prisons in your mind and you love to dwell there and let the enemy remind you of how useless he thinks you are. What does God say about you? If you don't spend time with Him, and allow Him to infiltrate your identity, others will define you. Then, you'll so comfortable in your mind cell you won't ever long for the feeling of freedom. You have the key to your escape and God wants to show you everlasting freedom. Don't let your tent be a place that holds you hostage. God has called you to an everlasting peace, and that peace is contagious. If your place of dwelling is a place of peace others will find their true Safe Haven in your presence because your presence remains in His presence. You could be the pathway that leads others straight to Christ. To help others we must help ourselves first by allowing Him into your tent. (Revelation 3:20) How strong is your tent today?

#StrengthenYourTent

### Release the Prisoner

You will extend your boundaries on all sides;

your people will get back the land

that the other nations now occupy.

Cities now deserted will be filled with people.

Isaiah 54:3

"Eww. I feel so disgusting. How I could I let him touch me like that? We were just supposed to be waiting until we got word if my grandma was going to be okay at the hospital. He talked me into it because; well he was older than me. He had known me all of my life, he was supposed to protect me. I was only nine at the time, but now that I am older I still feel guilty. I still feel like everything was my fault. I still feel like I should have told someone or that I should have stopped it. Now, I crave controlling relationships without even realizing I am in one until it feels like it's too late. Then, the cycle starts all over again. I wish that door never would have been opened. How do I say no? How do I stop the temptation from becoming too overwhelming? I hate him for that. I can't move on from this. Those memories are forever etched into my brain. I will always be dirty and gross for letting him touch me that way." Yuck!"

—Ella

Rape, molestation, and abusive relationships are surely a healing ministry all on their own. Any type of abuse holds such a stronghold, not only mentally and physically, but spiritually as well. Some form of abuse may have happened to you and you may presume that you are over it because you don't dwell on it as often as you used to, but honey, a little small trigger, like a scent or location, can bring you right back to the very place you thought you left behind.

Healing requires patience and time. I know for me personally, whenever a hurt happened to me, I wanted to be healed right away just so I could get it over with and move on. I hated the hurt. The hurt then turned to anger because I feel like I am good person, and I am nice so nothing bad should ever happen to me. I have learned now how wrong that concept is. Bad situations happen to even the best of people, but it's how you chose to overcome that really is the determining factor for your healing.

Let's just take a moment to set the tone. Thanksgiving used to be one of my favorite holidays. My family used to get together, laugh, joke, and of course eat just like any other family. Then times changed, we moved on, and now I think I have spent the last two Thanksgivings either alone, or around a bunch of people I barely knew. This past year (2016) God blessed me to spend it with a family from my hometown, and I could not have asked for a better holiday.

Let's just say that you are responsible for cooking the turkey for thanksgiving. That is your one and only responsibility for the entire day. It may only be one task, yet it is seemingly the most important one. How many thanksgivings have you attended where there was no turkey, unless you're a vegetarian of course, than your answer would be, pretty much, all of them!

You've waited until the last minute to try and cook this turkey, and you just throw it in the oven for one hour. Now, God forbid anyone would try this at home. We all know that a turkey takes hours to bake, unless you're from the south, like me, and love everything deep fried, but even that takes time! Your sixty minute turkey may look somewhat, and I am using somewhat very loosely here, decent. However, on the inside it is still raw and not edible. If anyone dares to eat your raw turkey they would become sick, right?

Healing is the same way when we rush our healing we become that sixty minute turkey. We look just about decent on the outside, but on the inside we are still raw. We wait until the last minute to try and do a fly by night healing. Perhaps, you want to get yourself together so you can date some guy because you think you're ready. Or so you can receive a certain job, but you know that place constantly reminds you of a past offense. You are sensitive to words and circumstances and if anyone dares to consume your presence, they will be negatively affected. Your healing seeps through your pores, it carries a weighty spirit and aura. People can feel when you are not healed, and they will not want to be around you. You know that feeling you have when you're around someone and their spirit is just off. There's no other way to explain it, it just does not feel welcoming. So if we know the backlash of being on the other side, we should want to get the healing process started right away, not only for others, but most importantly for you.

There was a period in my very own healing process from abandonment and rejection where I couldn't stand the sight of myself. I hated the way I looked. For a while, I thought because of the way I looked was the explanation for not receiving the love that I strongly desired. I hated the way I felt about myself, but I could not change it through my human power alone. I had wished over and over again to just be free from myself. I didn't even want to be around me, so I know for sure others did not dare want to step foot in my space. Being free and healed helps you become in tune with your true self. You can't run from yourself, so why not make yourself someone that you are proud to be?

I had a vision one day. Like I told you earlier, I have three older sisters, and I always wanted to be like them. They can surely attest to what I am about to say next, but I didn't start off as the girly girl that I somewhat am now. I say somewhat because I can be polishing my nails while yelling at a football game at the same time! Anyway, I never wanted to do my hair, or dress up when I was younger. Shoot, I barely cared if I was ashy! I just wanted to play. I was free and I didn't care what my sisters said about me, but one day all of that changed. My sister had a friend come to the house and her friend looked at me and said your little sister is ugly. Now, when my inner crew, being my mom and sisters, tried to tell me *"hey fix it up a bit"*, I didn't care. Yet, it was when an outsider came in and said *"hey you don't look so good"*, then I really started to believe what was being said about me. I carried that moment for many years.

In the vision that God gave me, I saw myself. I saw that free spirited little girl, who didn't want to comb her hair locked away in this dungeon. The dungeon was dark and cold and I saw myself sitting alone in the corner. The Lord said that when we hold onto memories and hurts we lock them away just like I had done with my younger self. He told me that I'd come and visit her often, but I tell her that she's ugly and unwanted. Every time I came to visit I brought nothing but negativity. For years, I had desired to be free from my insecurities. People in turn would tell me how beautiful I was, but I would just go visit the little girl and remind her of how ugly I thought she was.

The Lord told me in the vision that freedom is a choice. As soon as He spoke those words, I realized I had been holding a key the entire time. He told me that I had every opportunity to free this little girl, but instead I would remind her of her looks, and leave. All this time, I carried my freedom, yet I chose to be imprisoned by my mind and emotions. I decided that what others said about me held more value than what God said about me (Psalm 139:14).

I feel the Lord giving us the choice to be free, yet many of us just visit our inner prisoner and rehearse our feelings and what we have been told about ourselves. When we use that key to release our old selves and our old emotions we have the opportunity to extend our boundaries on all sides. Prison cells are only little rooms with inner walls that keep us from escaping, but if we free ourselves, with Christ's help, our territories are limitless. Believe or not, Abba is rooting for us! He died so that we could be free. Keeping our selves imprisoned tells Him that what He did for us on the cross wasn't good enough.

When we release the imprisoned, the boundaries are limitless. The word says that *"you will extend your boundaries on all sides and your people will get back the land that the other nations now occupy."* When we free ourselves, first, from personal bondage we will regain that hope and carefree spirit we once had before the hurt. Not only will we regain our confidence but we will get back the land that other nations occupy. I believe the land that the other nations occupy is the space, time, and energy we give the people who have wounded us deeply. We allow them to set up camp in our mind, hearts, and spirits, which gives them the freedom to roam and destroy us from the inside out. When we chose to forgive the hurts we release them into the hands of our Father, and we allow Him to take care of the rest. When we surrender our hurts, He fulfills us with His hope. Hallelujah to the King! He says that YOU WILL get back what your mama, your daddy, your abuser, your ex has occupied!

As we discussed earlier, whenever you encounter a person, good or bad, they leave a deposit. So if someone has left a negative deposit within you and it has swallowed up your peace whole, you have the authority through Jesus Christ to swiftly return to the sender! Won't He do it? *Cities now deserted will be filled with people.* The places you thought you would never go and the heights you thought you would never reach are now attainable. Someone may have expressed fervently to you that you would be absolutely useless in this lifetime. They may have said you were a good for nothin' nobody and that you would never amount to anything in your life. They basically proclaimed through their own eyes that the places you desired to go would be deserted, abandoned, and vacant. Yet they did not realize that you were hand selected by God before the beginning of time. They didn't realize that you are chosen, a royal priesthood, and He has given you hope beyond their accusations. (I Peter 2:9). They might not have known, but God knew (Isaiah 46:10). Places that were deserted or unreachable are now yours for the taking and not only will you be going, but the harvest that you produce will go with you, and most importantly He will go before you! Praise His holy name for hope and freedom (Hebrews 10:23). Unlock the cell and a release the prisoner.

#ForeverFree

### No Longer Ashamed

"Do not fear, for you will not be put to shame,

And do not feel humiliated or ashamed, for you will not be disgraced.

For you will forget the shame of your youth,

And you will no longer remember the disgrace of your widowhood.

Isaiah 54:4

"Before I truly became a Christ follower, I used to steal. I mean I would steal anything from makeup at stores to even underwear! I would do it mostly for the thrill, plus I didn't have as much money as my friends did. Their parents would pay for everything if they needed it. My mom wasn't around and it took my dad some serious convincing to let me have any kind of money. After that, I just bounced from house to house so I never felt comfortable asking for anything. I felt I was already a burden enough. No one ever knew I would steal though. It was my little secret, but I was highly ashamed. I dabbled in it even when I became to know Jesus in the early years. I remember one time in particular when I stole money from my job. I had no money after paying my bills so I didn't have enough to eat. I knew I wouldn't get paid for another two weeks, and at the time it was my only option. I was so ashamed of myself after I had spent the money on food, but, in my flesh, I was desperate. I wish trusting God to provide all of my needs would have been a priority for me back then like it is now."

—Laina

        I remember a season in my life when I lived in North Chicago, Illinois. My word, did it ever get freezing up there! I remember before my friend started giving me rides, I would stand plum frozen at my bus stop! Before I would step outside, I had to get myself prepared. I had to have on a big sweater, pants and leggings, a heavy jacket, my hat, gloves, thick socks, and boots, and on top of all that would be my backpack! Can you imagine prepping yourself with all of that gear and walking outside in the summer time? How suffocating and irrelevant would that be, right? You would look crazy, and you would be burning up!

        Taking the time and effort to dress for winter in the summer is like when we awaken daily and cloth ourselves with guilt and shame from past sins. If I were to wear that same jacket in mid-July in Atlanta, Georgia, where I reside now, I would just die! It is too much for the season that I am in. Before you came to know Christ for who He is, you wore the sin that was in style. Period. You had fallen short (Romans 3:23). When you came to know Him, you became clothed in His righteousness and those garments of the past are no longer in season (Romans 5:17; Isaiah 61:10; 2 Corinthians 5:17).

Not only would the winter attire be out of style, it would be extremely heavy to carry around, and let's not to mention the suffocation. Winter jackets are not made with light material for obvious reasons, and guilt and shame were not designed to be as lightweight as freedom and righteousness. Jesus said that my yolk is easy and my burden is light (Matthew 11:30). When Christ died for us guilt and shame died along with Him. He rose again on the third day but guilt and shame were swallowed by the grave. The evil twins were never meant to be resurrected in us because they exist to kill our peace and our joy, which is ultimately rooted in Christ. If you are searching for peace and joy elsewhere then you will find yourself constantly unsatisfied.

Do you know of someone that always likes to remind you of your past sins? They'll say things like remember when you used to mess around with so and so? Remember when you used to get drunk every weekend and act plum crazy? Remember this and remember that? Eventually you will have to answer. It can either go one of two ways. One, when guilt and shame ( aka grandma and auntie) come knocking you answer and willingly allow them to come in and before you know it, your thoughts are running rapid then, boom, you are clothed for winter in the summertime. Or, guilt and shame (this time it may be Ray-Ray and them) can come knocking and you tell them that the person that they are looking for no longer resides in that place. The choice is yours. You are never obligated to stay the same person forever. It's ok to outgrow yourself every once in a while.

When mail comes to your house and it has someone else's name on it, you don't keep it and store it in your house to collect junk, you return it back to the sender! That's exactly what happens when you chose to entertain others, who are ultimately trying to take the heat from their shortcomings off them and place it onto you. You're collecting junk mail, and instead of tossing it you waste time hoarding something that doesn't belong to you in the first place. When you give your life to Christ your old self dies away and your new being is made alive and well. You've made the decision to give your life to Christ, so therefore it no longer belongs to you. I do not give others the permission to ruin my peace. I know it may be hard at times to keep within your character; however Jesus was talked about too. What makes you think that we would be exempt?

I don't know about you, but guilt always seems to rear its ugly head when the sun goes down. I love my sleep more than anything! Those who truly know me will tell you that is a true fact about me! I heard that you grow taller when you sleep; I should be like 11 feet 5 inches by now! However, past mistakes tend to creep into my mind in the middle of the night as soon as I get relaxed. I have learned to just send that thought to the throne of grace and take my tail right on to sleep. What good is it to waste time on a thought or mistake when it has already been forgiven?! Make every thought obedient to Christ (2 Corinthians 10:5). So if Jesus says that all your sins are forgiven, then that's the final verdict on the case! Not only are you forgiven, but you are blessed (Romans 4:7-8). Respond, I am the righteousness of God because Christ Jesus died for me (2 Corinthians 5:21) and I am free from bondage, sin and shame (John 8:36). Proclaim it boldly because that's who you are. If we do not know **who** you are and **whose** you are, then someone else will make that decision for you.

Have you noticed throughout the bible when Jesus approached someone shamed by others, He didn't condemn them, He showed them sincere compassion? That is still how He treats us today. The God of the bible is still relevant today, and His character is still the same (Hebrews 13:8). So, if you feel that you are unable to fully open up to Him or trust Jesus completely out of fear of His response He will respond with grace, love, and compassion. That's why He comforts us with His words "Do not fear, you will not be put to shame, you will not be humiliated." We do not serve a God who takes pleasure in putting His children on "blast". He will bring conviction for your sin, but He does not identify you by your sin. He doesn't sip or share the tea! That is not in His character. He loves us. He loves you. He wants to take the shame you have been carrying and exchange it for His peace, and eternal life.

If you are still carrying around shame and guilt, it may be for a sin you have not confessed. However, you do not have to keep confessing the same sin over and over. Some of you may be like *"Lord please forgive me for that piece of gum I stole when I was five."* Now, every time you see a piece of gum in the checkout line, you are reminded of that moment and you confess it each time. That is not necessary. God forgets our sin once we confess them. He tosses it as far as the east is from the west. (Psalms 103:12). He promises are the same for you. At times during this walk, I would only think that certain promises pertained to certain followers. I felt like there was some type of ranking system, but it doesn't work like that at all. His promises apply to you if you have been a Christian for 10 years or 10 seconds. Once you are adopted into His kingdom, the benefits are automatic. Can you imagine if you adopted a child, and then made that child wait five years for them to receive the same love or protection as the children you naturally birthed or could have birthed?

He says that *"we will forget the shame of our youth."* I was speaking with one of my mentors recently because I was going through a few situations amongst my job. I was asked to recall what happened on May 27, 2009. I was told that it was a very important day. He kept asking me, but I was so confused, and I really tried hard to remember, but nothing came to mind. After coming to the conclusion that I wouldn't remember, then I was told that's how God looks at our sin. He does not even recall it!

He also promises that *"you will forget the disgrace of your widowhood."* Widowhood simply means the period during which a woman remains a widow, or unmarried due to the death of her spouse. The definition is pretty self-explanatory actually. Now when we lived in sin, we were married to it. We made a covenant with it, and we did any and everything that we could to make sure that we did not break up. We loved our sin. We were one until Christ's death parted us. Then, when we became introduced to Christ, sin had to die within us and around us, right? However, we did not know how to be a faithful spouse to Christ in the beginning. When you died to your old way of life, Did you lose friends during this time period? Did your atmosphere start to shift? Did people begin to slander your name and tell the town your business now that you are no longer in a covenant with what they like? Does it all sound vaguely familiar?

When sin became dead to us, it was a transitional period. One, where we no longer enjoyed or are enticed by our relationship with sin, but we hadn't fully discovered the goodness of Christ. In that time of widowhood, many situations can take place, some of which I have mentioned above. However, once we discover the goodness of Christ the pain of losing friends, the loneliness, the hurts, and even the cravings to continue to dabble in sin no longer have a lasting impact, because we were introduced to and fell in love with God, Himself, and to God's grace.

I am not a mother, but I hear stories all the time of hard labor and the indescribable amounts of pain, but once they saw their baby for the first time the pain was a distant memory. The pain didn't matter because it birthed a love that cannot be quenched. I imagine that is exactly how God feels about you and I: His beloved Daughters. We caused Him pain when we nailed Him to the cross and beat Him unmercifully when we sinned against Him. We broke His heart when we yelled *"We want Barrabas"* (Luke 23:18-23). Physically, we weren't with the crowd that day, but spiritually we chose sin over the Savior. Now, that we have confessed our sins to Him and have been adopted into His family, He looks upon us just as a mother looks upon her newborn baby. We are beautiful to Him. We are loved unconditionally by Him, and the pain we caused Him is no longer a factor in our relationship with Him. Some parts of life are just worth forgetting.

#Unashamed

### I Now Pronounce You Husband & Wife

"For your maker is your husband, the Lord of hosts is His name, and the Holy One of Israel is your redeemer, the God of the whole earth he is called."

Isaiah 54:5

"Sometimes, it is hard being single in a room full of married women and women who are in committed relationships. As much as I do love to hang around mature women who are married, it's a constant reminder of what I currently don't have. I want some of their relational wisdom to rub off on me because you can never learn too much. I do dream about the day I get married, and what type of wife I will be. I get excited, and it is one of my heart's deepest desires to become a kingdom partner to someone. However, it is really difficult not finding the right one. I know, as a woman, you aren't supposed to be searching, but it gets lonely some days. I go on a couple of dates, and sometimes, not often, I may find myself seriously involved with someone only for it not to last very long. I guess I'll just keep waiting for what God has in store for me, but for now, let me get off Pinterest."

—Sacha

Marriage is a beautiful part of life, and it is also a healthy desire. However, if you are single like me, it can become easy to make something that is healthy, unhealthy really quickly by how much of your desire for it consumes you. Desiring to be married is not a sin, but making it an idol is (Exodus 20:5-6). You dream about it constantly. Every detail of the wedding is planned via Pinterest, and yet there is no groom in sight! Perhaps you have a potential someone in mind, and you're constantly checking their social media pages a million times throughout the day, just to see what he's doing. I am about to break somebody's heart. Honey, if he has not pursued you, he is not thinking about you right now. I have learned that most guys really do have a one track mind. If they truly want something or someone, they will go after them. So stop checking. He still works in the same place, he still does the same activities, and he is still not pursuing you right now. Take the extra time to focus on a goal that you have set for yourself. Focus on God right now, enjoy your single season, and prepare for what's to come next.

Before any life altering decisions are made, He gives us time to prepare, whether we realize it or not. Hear me out. How many times have seemingly small steps of faith effected your decisions for grand leaps of faith? God knows our very desires, because He created them. I think at times Christians think that they created their own desires. No ma'am, Pam! The reason you may not like peas is because God created you that way. The reason that you love chocolate is because God created you that way. He knows us inside and out and from top to bottom, from our dislikes to our fondest desires. If you are a single woman, your time to be a wife is not when you become a wife to an earthly vessel, it is now. The scriptures say that our Maker is our husband. He is the perfect example of love.

Now that you have come to the realization that you are in a covenant, as His wife, are you faithful to Him? How can we expect and "plan" to be a good wife to an earthly man, who is expected to let us down sometime in this life, and we cannot even stay faithful to a God who has never left us nor forsaken us? Am I saying you should be perfect? No, because that is impossible, but there are areas in your life that can be addressed and changed. You don't spend time with Him like you should. You view your quiet time as a chore and have affairs with fantasies and dreams of other men, and all the while He is beckoning you to spend time and cling to Him. So you are not alone, you are just lonely, and you're doing meaningless tasks to fill the void when you could be made completely whole by seeking the Maker!

I spoke earlier in the beginning of our journey about wanting to ultimately becoming like the Proverbs 31 woman. The passage of Proverbs 31 does not jump right in complementing this noble woman. Oh no, it starts with a lesson that King Lemuel's mother taught him. Now, we all are aware that mama knows best, especially when it comes to her boys! She warns him against women who ruin kings. (Proverbs 31: 1-7) Single women, perhaps, as much as you think you want a man; you have a mouth or habits (partying, drinking, cussing, poor saving skills, etc) within your life that will ruin a king. We are called to be help meet for our Kingdom Partners not a headache. (Genesis 2:18). His very own mama is telling him to look for the opposite of what you may be bringing to the table! Times may have changed, but the love and knowledge of a mother has not! It's time for a change for you, is it not? God absolutely adores us, yet He also absolutely adores your future spouse as well. God won't bring him into a situation that will harm him, remember that. This concept of living is not only for your future spouse, but most importantly; it is for your Husband now: God. Do you talk to God or at Him? Are you speaking life into others around you or are you constantly speaking death?

I do want to take the time to explain what I mean about preparation. Our time here on earth is **not** meant to prepare us for another human being. Our time here on earth is **not** meant to be spent pleasing another earthen vessel. I know as young girls playing dress up and house that our tone for life was set to be just a wife and mother to another human, but our time here on earth is meant to prepare us for our KING, and to fulfill His will. If/When God calls you to your Adam, your preparation for the coming of the King does not cease. You can continue to be all that God has called you to be in order to walk alongside your Kingdom Partner and the two of you will ultimately fulfill God's will on earth for His kingdom. That's why it is important to know your purpose so that you won't be dating around trying to find someone to fit your fly-by-the-wind lifestyle. That will only accomplish confusion, heartache, and time wasted. While you are betrothed to Christ alone in this season, it's the time to set habits and learn who you are in Christ, first and foremost. This is the time to seek Him wholeheartedly with no distractions. This is the time to allow yourself to be rooted in Him, while learning your purpose through Him and His will for your life. You are so caught up in meeting your wishlist to build-a-husband, are you even prepared to be a wife? Could you go to war through prayer for your family?

I always let others know up front, that if we become friends I will give you the honest truth whether you are right or wrong. When you are right, I will celebrate with you, and when you are wrong, I will help you get it right. Then there's this part of me that when you're in trouble or being attacked, I will go to war for you. I will war in prayer on your behalf. I will war in worship on your behalf. You will never have to fight alone.


So picture this, you become married, but during your single season, you wasted all of the precious time that God gave you complaining about being single, instead of working towards being entirely what God has called you to be. The honeymoon is now over, and you are wondering why your husband doesn't do the cute antics he used to do, he works overtime, and you become lonely even though you are not physically alone. You begin to nag your husband day and night because you are wanting him to fill a void that he was never created to fill in the first place. You have been programmed to idolize dust, trying to make him wear the King's crown that he was never intended to wear in the first place. Because your firm foundation was not in Christ, you are constantly angry and disappointed. You have made a man made of clay an idol. You worship his words and actions. You seek him to fill your inner desires, and when he lets you down you feel all the more lost, clueless, and hopeless.

Thou shall not have any other gods before me, declares the Lord (Exodus 20:3).

When we make God our husband first, our number one priority, the ails of marriage or even life when they come, and they will because life is not a fairytale, we will have a place of refuge. Don't waste this time in your single season. Learn to serve and listen in this season. We are a part of a generation that boasts about themselves and only listens to respond. Listen to others needs outside of your own and learn to be compassionate, and heed to authority and instruction.

Submission is not to be a curse upon us, women but a blessing. When we fully submit to the Lord, we can fully submit to our future husbands. If you are married, and submission is an issue for you, ask yourself this question: How do I submit to the Lord? How to I act when God is giving me instruction? Are you serving Him? Submission is not intended to be dark cloud of authority, but an umbrella of protection.

Although I am not married yet, being around couples has shown me that the answer to any healthy relationship is to become a servant. It starts today. When you learn to serve you learn do so even when you don't feel like it. There may come a time in your relationship where you may not want to help your spouse because of the attitude he gave you earlier that day. Are you just going to serve only when you get what you want? Is that how you treat God? You only serve at the church when you know you'll get something in return. How you are in your single season, reflects directly how you'll be married. When you wake up, get into the habit of asking the Lord what you can do to serve Him today. Spend time with Him and discover what makes Him smile. Date your spouse. When we serve others it stops becoming solely about you alone.

One aspect about our generation that I have noticed is how selfish we are. We love for everything to be all about us. We have a 'me' mentality all the time. That type of mindset will not work for any relationship. Ever. When some of you think about serving, you cringe. This concept may take a while to grasp, but once it takes root, it is life altering. When you serve another person, and they serve you, while you both are serving the Lord, there is a healthy balance formed. When you serve yourself and then you want your partner to serve you as well, there's clearly an imbalance there. Something is off, and it does not add up. Who will serve your partner? Don't give the devil any cracks to destroy any of your relationships by giving your partner an out to look for acceptance and servitude elsewhere!

In the bible, Paul speaks about how it is better to be alone than to be with someone. He says this because when we do become involved with someone our attention is split between the Lord and our families. If you know you have a desire to be married, why not spend as much time with the Lord with no distractions as you possibly can? Don't worry He will send the right one for you in due time, so enjoy this time with Him alone. I know that life comes with its challenges, and we are seemingly distracted by work, school, and other life issues, however, it is so imperative to make Him number one over it all now! I don't want this to be a chapter where you use God. I mean use in terms of taking advantage of His presence to get a spouse. That is not the point. You should never get into the habit of spending time with Him for His **presents**, but you should love to spend time alone with Him for His **presence**. Everything you will ever need dwells there. Learn to love your maker for who He is to you, and for who He is overall. Learn to hear His voice. Learn to fall in love with Him and Him alone. Learn to be with Him. Learn His heartbeat, and what makes Him happy, because He is your life support, and He will never let you down.

Within the verse, it says that the Lord is your redeemer. It is not too late to start over with God. If He can create the heavens and the earth, He can redeem the way that you view Him. He can redeem the status of your relationship with Him. He surely can redeem the times. When your relationship with Him, who is our foundation, is secure, you will know how to love with a Christ like kind of love in all areas of your life. The more you spend time with Him, the more you'll want to stay in His presence. So what? You tripped coming down the aisle. Turn back around, start over, fix your veil, and walk boldly towards your Maker, who is your Husband. #HereComesTheBride

## The Griever

"The Lord will call you back as if you were a wife deserted and distressed in spirit—

a wife who married young, only to be rejected," says your God. Isaiah 54:6

"Gosh, I feel like I can't keep my life together. One good thing happens and then ten bad things happen and destroys all hope of consistency. I pray and seek the Lord, and I feel like I hear Him, but maybe I don't at all. I see all of these good things happening for other people and I am wondering when it will be my turn. I feel like my life is equivalent to being in a line with other people, and everyone who is in front of me and behind me gets exactly what they need while I am being told to step to the side. Then, that puts me in a place of do I really love God for who He is or for what He can give me? Will I continue to seek Him though He is stripping me of everything I thought I wanted? What is happening? I am so confused. I am angry with Him. I already have a hard time trusting Him, and I still have to trust Him even after everything I worked hard for is gone? I want to quit so badly, but there is still a sliver of hope within me that maybe my life will somehow work itself out or He will come through Himself, right? Maybe He hasn't forgotten about me.

-Eden

There are different types of grief, and throughout my life I have personally experienced the many stages that go along with it. One is the grief of physical death. When I lost my grandfather in 2014, I didn't know how I was going to make it. His transition happened following the loss of my cousin in 2012 and the loss of my uncle in 2013. It hurt me greatly because I was close to him, and though he didn't know who I was because of his dementia diagnosis, I still loved him for the memories we created before he got sick. I loved him because he never showed favoritism amongst his grandchildren. He loved us all the same. I had experienced the opposite affect from my grandmother on the other side of my family. She always made it known that only a few of my cousins were her favorite, and that hurt me immensely growing up and even now it still stings when I experience it. With my grandad, he never made any of us grandchildren feel that level of hurt or rejection. He always had his video camera to capture all of our proudest moments. He never captured just one grandchild, he got us all. He was so proud of all of us, and that made us feel good knowing that we were his.

At his funeral, there was a moment of grief that I had never experienced before. I knew he was gone, but it hadn't registered within me that he had actually passed away. Every time my aunt, cousins and I would go to the store or anywhere for that matter, he was always trucking along behind us. He would walk at his own pace, his over 6 foot frame just tagging along. So the day of his funeral, I just knew he would just show up after a while. I thought maybe he was just walking slowly somewhere. At the church, I saw his body in the casket, but my mind still couldn't wrap around the fact that he was actually gone. I kissed him and his body was ice cold, but he was still alive to me. My emotions went through their normal motions of crying when the casket closed and speeches from family and others as we remembered him that day. I cried. I cried a lot.

When we went to the gravesite to bury him, the preacher confirmed with us that this would be his final resting place. That reality made my heart sink a little bit. Everyone laid down their rose, and it was over. As we all continued to walk up the hill to the cars that brought us there, I remember walking slower than everyone else, and then suddenly the chatter of family and friends slowly began to fade. I turned around to realize that my granddaddy was not behind us tagging along. I frantically looked around for him only to find myself back at his casket and grief overcame me like a rushing flood. I will never forget that day. I will never forget that feeling.

Grief doesn't just come when someone we love passes on. Grief can come when we lose someone who is alive as well. I know I spoke briefly of my mother earlier, but the moment I started to grieve her existence was a very hard time in my life.

This level of grief was also my first time experiencing depression. If you have ever experienced depression, you know that it comes with different faces every time it comes to visit.

I never really got over the emotional abandonment my mother gave after she married her husband. I really needed her. I mean, every girl needs her mother in her life. There were a lot of lessons that I taught myself. For example how to do my hair, how to keep myself up to par during that time of the month, what items would be best to use during that time, etcetera, and boys. Oh, gosh the boys. I never knew who to talk to about the guys I liked. She never called on my birthday or Christmas after I made the decision to go live with my father, and that was hard and painful. So from the age of eleven to seventeen our relationship was nonexistent. I would pretend in my mind that I had the perfect family, even though I was going from family member to family member.

When I moved to Adairsville, Georgia to live with my grandmother, I was 17 years old. I was a senior, a cheerleader, in the yearbook club, and I had a job. I was so excited to be a part of all these activities. School itself was mediocre; I mean I had always been an average student, but being a part of after school activities made the year go by so much quicker! Thank God, because I was so ready to graduate! Although I will always consider Adairsville home, this was the place where my feelings of abandonment enhanced.

I never felt as loved as my cousins had. I knew growing up, my sisters and I, could only visit Adairsville because we moved so much. However, when I permanently resided there that was the excuse to why I wasn't treated like my cousins. I always felt left out at home, so I always made sure I had somewhere to be afterschool; hence, the many activities that I was in. I was always out with friends or working to not have to feel so rejected.

One day, I got a call from my mother saying how much she missed me, and how we should rekindle our relationship, and how she wanted me to move to Mississippi to be with her. Even though I was a part of all these great opportunities and had made many friends, I could not pass up the opportunity to rekindle my relationship with my mother. I missed her, and I finally felt that it was my turn to be loved like any other child should. So, I packed all of my belongings and moved back to Mississippi to be with her.

It was all well and good in the beginning. We caught up and we laughed, but that didn't last too long. The strict discipline became all too familiar again. I remember living there before and how my sister and I were made to wear skirts full time due to religious purposes. This time, I had the choice of wearing skirts or pants, and I chose to wear pants full time because I felt comfortable. I had just gotten saved the year before at age 16, and I felt that making the decision to wear pants would not be a life or death situation for my faith. For some reason, it didn't cause as much friction as I thought. I was asked for important documents such as my social security number and card and my identification card. I trusted her, and didn't think of it as suspicious because she was my mother so I gave it to her. I was doing well at my new school, and I really started thinking seriously about college. My sister, Tory, helped me fill out applications to one of my favorite schools, The University of Tennessee-Knoxville. For some reason, I was just drawn to this school. I had loved it ever since I used to watch Candace Parker play on television with my sister, Shekia.

I remember the night I got accepted. I received an email earlier that day, but didn't read it until late that night. When I had seen that Tennessee had accepted me I was overjoyed! I went and woke my mom and stepdad up and told them that I had been accepted. Now, you would think that any parent would be excited about their child being accepted into one of the greatest schools in the nation, but sadly, I got the opposite reaction. They were upset and I didn't understand why. They kept trying to talk me into going to a local college, the University of South Alabama. I remember distinctly telling them that I wanted to go to UT and tried to convince them of how great of a school it was.

The next line from my stepfather is one I will never forget. He said *"yeah you go, but if anything happens to you while you are out there don't call us."* I looked at my mother and she just sat there and nodded. I was so confused and angry! How could they not be excited? That night I made a vow to myself that I would finish out my senior year strong at Moss Point High School, and leave as soon as I graduated, and I did just that.

I graduated high school on May 21, 2010 and left Mississippi to go back to Georgia on May 23rd, with the help of my sister, Tory. I grieved my mother when I left her. I felt sad that she didn't want to be a part of my journey....again. That summer my sister, my aunt and uncle, and I got what I needed to head to UT. I remember the week before, my aunt had surgery on her stomach, but that didn't stop her from moving me into my dorm. I will never forget that because it meant so much to me that she would do that despite her pain.

I loved the college life! I loved being held more responsible for my success. Not long after being at UT, I started getting notices about my payments. Now, it was my understanding that my school was paid for, but the bursar's office was saying otherwise. I called the social security office from which my payments were supposed to be coming from to make sure everything was set in place. My sisters and I all received checks from them when we turned 18, due to our mother being hurt from the military. When I called, I was angered to find out that my check was gone. The operator told me that I had come to make sure my check got sent to a specific address. When I asked her the address, I noticed that it was my mother's address. I told the operator that it was not me who came to the office and that I needed to speak with someone immediately. She informed me that I had brought in the proper identification and I had signed for it, so there wasn't much that she could do for me. I recalled the times, I let my mother scan and copy my id cards, and how much we looked alike so it surely would have been easy for her to make this transaction. My heart was crushed and I was perplexed about the whole situation. Later in life, I found out that all she needed was for me to be living with her for her to even have access to the money as my guardian. Hence, the phone call I got about wanting to "repair our relationship." Not long after, UT told me I had 48 hours to move out of my dorm because I didn't have the funds to stay in school. I was humiliated. How could the Lord let this happen to me? How come I didn't have a loving mother who wanted the best for me? The anger overtook me, but thankfully I was able to find a place within 24 hours. The Lord, in spite of my anger, provided a way for me to stay in a house with two athletes, who were so sweet. I literally had nothing to contribute to the house when I moved in except for my clothes, and that made me feel like a complete failure even more.

I worked two jobs and walked to them every single day. The walk took me about an hour each way. One started at 6 in the morning until 2 pm and the other started at 4 pm until midnight, and I would walk home at night and do it all over again the next morning. During that time, I was still a part of on campus activities. One in particular was a Christian organization called Chi Alpha. Those people loved me back to life, and I will always be grateful for that. Honestly, it was hard to be a part of that group because I was so fragile, and they seemed so full of life. The first year that I went I cried at every service, and I didn't know why. I later learned it was because my spirit warrior was grieving. I was wounded and broken. I was grieving the loss of my living mother. I was grieving the loss of my education and the dreams I had hoped to accomplish through my new found knowledge. I was grieving the loss of all hope as I had known it.

Sometimes in life we grieve the losses that seem to be so tangible. We marry our dreams and our deepest desires only to be rejected by them, sometimes through no fault of our own, and it hurts. It cuts worse than a knife. It penetrates worse than a speeding bullet, and some days we think we will never be able to get out of bed because we are so emotionally drained and distraught that any sign of hope is foreign to us.

As I am writing this, I am emotionally drained. I am tired....again. My warrior's armor feels heavier than ever today. After years of trying to get back into school, I was accepted to Kennesaw State University in Kennesaw, Georgia. It is increasingly becoming one of the largest schools in the state. I was so happy and thankful to be able to start my education over again after my stint in Tennessee. I trusted God to provide every penny for school, and this one was thousands of dollars cheaper than my last school because I was now officially considered an in state student.

Everything was going very well. Doors were opening left and right, I was getting amazing grades in school, I got a house, I got a car. It all looked well until one day when I went to do my homework, ALL of my classes had been canceled. I received a call telling me that my scholarship didn't go through. This scholarship required me to have graduated from a Georgia high school, and the only way I was able to receive is if I had done thirty credit hours at KSU first. Also, my FASFA did not supply me with money due to the debauchery at Tennessee. So the only way to move forward was to pay roughly four thousand dollars up front to attend for the remaining of the semester.

The rejection feels all too familiar. I want to quit. I am writing this in real time because I want to allow those who may be feeling this way right now to have someone that they can relate to. Although, I want to quit, and I want to give up right this second, I can't. I stop and think of you. How will you make it through if I just quit at chapter 6? Who else won't be touched if I stop on this page, this paragraph, this sentence, or this word? I believe God put me in this position to help all of you. I had to experience grief all over again to fully relay His healing power to all of you. I don't know what He is going to do. I don't know how this story ends, but as much as I want to give up on Him and you, I can't.

I am choosing today to believe this verse from our passage in Isaiah.

*"The Lord will call you back as if you were a wife deserted and distressed in spirit—*

*a wife who married young, only to be rejected," says your God. Isaiah 54:6*

Will you believe with me? He is calling me back. He is calling you back too. He is in constant pursuit of us. It's okay to be angry and confused, but we cannot give up here. I am not telling you this just as a cliché, I am literally walking through it one little step at a time. I have to tell myself to get out of bed just like you. The dark days want to strangle me as well, but I have to put one foot in front of the other, and trust Him even when I don't want to anymore. I am learning to believe God for myself and I am believing for you too. Are you in that place too? Join together. Grieve the loss, but lets not settle there. *"Do not grow weary in well doing for in the proper time we will receive a harvest if we do not give up."*

*(Galatians 6:9)*

#GrieveJustDontGiveUP

### Just For a Brief Moment

For a brief moment I abandoned you, but with deep compassion I will bring you back.

8 In a surge of anger I hid my face from you for a moment, but with everlasting kindness I will have compassion on you," says the Lord your Redeemer.

Isaiah 54:7-8

"Lord where are You? I have cried out to You day and night. I can't see You. I have to force myself to worship You at church because I feel like I don't know you anymore and it doesn't come as naturally. I know I shouldn't have to force it, but I feel like it is hard for me right now. You say You'll never leave me or forsake me, but I feel so alone. I know that I have strayed away, but I'm back now. Have I lost you forever? I miss You, but I feel as though everyone around me is connected to You but me. Where are You?

-Anna

What do you think about most often? What occupies your head space? Is it the crush you've liked since high school or your current relationship? Is it money or possessions? Is it your spouse and kids? It can be a number of things, right? Anything we think of or love more than God is an idol. We spend time with those thoughts and strategies of dreams and success more than we spend time with Him, and then we turn around and wonder why we don't hear Him like we should or like we used to. If you spent time with someone, you would know them. You would know what they liked and disliked. Their voice and habits would become familiar to you and you would even know what makes them happy or sad. What if one day you just stopped spending time with that person? A significant amount of time has passed, years even. Would you know them then? Would the things you once had known about them still be the same? That's how it is on this walk with Christ.

One day you become introduced to Him and you are on fire for Him. You want to spend every waking moment reading your bible, praying, and learning more about Him. You get to know who He is. Then one day the readings and prayer times become shorter and shorter and next thing you know you are too busy. You become occupied with other things and other voices, to the point where you don't recognize your first love. I'm sure on this walk this has happened to us all at one point or another. Or maybe you are just starting on this journey and this is where you currently find yourself.

Being a Christian is having a personal relationship with God. How would you feel if you went above and beyond in a relationship to have your significant other only spend one day out of the week to acknowledge you? Or only come to you when they needed something? Or rush through spending quality time together because they are too busy, but at least they did it, right? I am sure God feels the same hurt you would feel if that were you. However, in reality, that's how we treat Him. A whole week will go by without spending time with Him, and then on Sundays you dress your best to impress other people. You go through the motions of lifting your hands during worship and putting your money in the offering plate and the oh, so common *"yes sister so and so, I will be sure to keep you in my prayers this week,"* only to become so busy that we don't even do it.

How familiar does that become and then Monday-Saturday our lives our occupied by your true loves- your fantasies, your job, your education, and your relationships with humans and social media. As we all know God is way bigger than anything we could ever fathom. We see him as bigger than our issues, bigger than our universe, but His frame is also bigger than ours, His heart is bigger than ours and His emotions run deeper than ours ever could, because He is the Creator of ALL things, even feelings.

Imagine how much it hurts Him when we spend time with him just too impress other people as if He's some trophy God. We treat Him as if He's something that makes us look good. As if He is worthy to have us and not the other way around. We treat him as if He is some kind of fashion accessory that we can tack on to our outfits to make them pop. Our minds are not fixed on him, and we love his hand more than his heart. I use the word we because at times, I am included in these realities too.

For a brief moment He abandoned us, and I totally understand why He would leave us in our mess. Sometimes we question where God is in our lives, but we haven't taken the time to sit with him and hear his heart towards us or our situations. Think of another scenario like this, you set a time and place to meet with a friend every day, and that friend constantly reassures you that they will make that meeting, however that day comes along and the time to meet approaches rapidly without even a phone call from your friend. Finally you become tired of waiting and you leave.

The next day your friend calls and doesn't even apologize for not showing up they just talk about how awful their day went and how they need something very important from you. They read off a laundry list of request they need from you! Then they promise to meet you, same place, same time, the next day. So again, you wait patiently for them to arrive only to have the same results; a no show with a laundry list of request for the next day.

That's how we treat our God, we promise to make time for Him, but find ourselves way too busy with peasant activities than to spend quality time with the King, Himself. Then we 'pray' and ask Him for all the things we want or need. I put the word pray in quotation marks for a specific reason. Prayer is considered to be a means of communication. A good friend of mine once told me that when we pray and make it all about us it's like calling up someone on the phone talking about ourselves, talking about the weather, and then we ask our friend how they're doing, but before we have time to hear what they have to say we hang up. Prayer is being in constant communication with the Father. That means not only speaking, but **listening**. When we ask Him for something do we not want to hear the answer? We have to give him time to respond back to us. I call that mastering the spirit of hush. Be quiet and let him speak to you.

Try becoming a habitual listener. When you cry out to Him, He will answer you, if you learn to listen. I've learned on this walk that God is quite funny. He loves to make His children smile and He loves to make them happy. I have learned to listen to Him in such a way, that there are roads that I won't go down because He says not to. I have learned to incorporate Him in every part of my life- from what to wear to where I go to lunch. That may sound silly to you, but it is important. Every aspect of my life is important to Him, and He wants to be included. This theme in this generation of being Ms. Independent is so overrated. I don't want to do this life alone without my Heavenly Father.

So can we really be upset with God for turning his back on us for just a brief moment? It is like when you give someone who has treated you unfairly or who doesn't appreciate your time to realize their actions. When someone continuously takes advantage of you without reciprocating your actions in return would that not be frustrating?

The Lord says that He calls us back with compassion because He loves you despite your actions towards Him. He loves you and although He is the almighty God, He is not exempt from emotional pain, but He doesn't want anyone to perish so He still endures. Even after the pain of the cross, Jesus knew that He would still be rejected thereafter, that type of love is deep and unmatched. He has never abandoned us, but we have abandoned Him time and time again. He doesn't force His love on you; Jesus wants you to choose Him on purpose!

I had a vision one day when I was in Montana for the summer in 2012. I had learned what freedom truly looked and felt like. In the basement where we stayed, the directors had turned one of the rooms into a prayer room. Throughout the summer, it increasingly became my favorite place. In my vision, God lead me out of a dark cave into hills and fields of grass that were pure green. I saw mountains, and rivers and the scenery was the most beautiful place I had ever seen. God told me that a tree in the middle of the field was our place. That is where we would meet and talk, laugh, and spend time together. Now on the other side of our tree, just a walk away, that dark cave and forest was still ever present. It was like He was giving me a choice to stay with Him or return to the dark cave.

A couple of months after I left Montana, I hit a rough spot. I was really looking for God and hoping that He would hear my prayers. I was going through the motions at church, when one day He showed me in another vision of me at the edge of that dark cave, and a little ways across the field, I saw God sitting at our spot patiently waiting for me. I began to run to Him and He looked so happy to have me back. He didn't yell and He wasn't upset, He just treated me like I had never left.

He is everlastingly kind towards us, and His grace and mercy endures forever (Psalm 136:1). So what have you put in place of meeting with God? If you feel that you have not heard from Him lately, check your heart and then check your schedule. Are you using God's glory to bring benefit to yourself? He won't be upset with you forever. He is the creator of emotions and perhaps you have grieved Him, but when you come to acknowledge and confess your mess ups, He is faithful to forgive you of all unrighteousness (I John 1:9). He will redeem the time that we have wasted on thoughts or actions or even people, who in the grand scheme of things, don't really matter. He redeems our emotional lack. He redeems our selfishness with more of Him. What's the good news? He is always willing to allow us to return back to Him. If this particular chapter has caused you to look deep within yourself pray this prayer with me:

"Abba, I have abandoned you, and I know that you have, for a brief moment, allowed me see the error of my ways. I love you and I am sorry for treating you unlike the Holy One that you are. You deserve my worship, my praise, and my very life. Every breath that I breathe comes directly from You. I thank You for your everlasting compassion and kindness. Show me where I can improve on our relationship. Show me what needs to be taken out of my life and be replaced with more of You. I love you. Amen."

#NowListen

### Promises

"To me this is like the days of Noah, when I swore that the waters of Noah would never again cover the earth. So now I have sworn not to be angry with you, never to rebuke you again. Though the mountains be shaken and the hills be removed, yet my unfailing love for you will not be shaken nor my covenant of peace be removed,"

says the Lord, who has compassion on you.

Isaiah 54: 9-10

"There was a time when I was so depressed that I counted out twenty-two pink little pills representing my twenty-two worthless years on this earth. I just couldn't take it anymore. I never felt so alone in all of my life. I heard the devil say just take them no one will care. I truly believed that in my heart that no one would give a crap if I left this earth, so that's what I did. I took them. I swallowed them all. Within less than five minutes, the room begin to spin and I all of my limbs became instantly numb. I remember taking a blurry crawl to my bed and laying there knowing that this was going to be the end. That I was going to die that very day. That was until I woke up. I couldn't speak to save my life all of my words just sounded like mumbo jumbo. At some points, I would start to say something and my thought would leave me instantly. It had to be all God because I went to work that night and no one questioned my crazy antics. Maybe because I was still considered the new girl and they were still trying to feel me out. A virus started going around at work so when I threw up everything I had ever eaten I blamed it on the virus and not the fact that I desperately tried to end my life a few hours before. No one ever knew what I had done. I went to church that following week and I felt so ashamed. It felt like everyone knew what I had done. I looked around and saw everyone worshipping and I thanked God for letting me worship with his children even after trying to take the life that He'd given me. In that moment I saw Him rise from His throne and say "you are my child too", and in the midst of everyone worshipping Him, He pointed to me and said "you are the one that I want." I cried really hard at that service because there was a peace I had never known. I knew it was Him that spared my life. Sad part is, sometimes, I still think about doing it again when times get really rough. I want to truly trust Him with my life and everything in it.

—Elizabeth

How many times have you done something that you know is not pleasing in His sight, and then you automatically get this heart wrenching feeling that God hates you? The good news (because if you haven't noticed, there's always the Good News) He doesn't hate us. God's love for us is eternal because He sent His very own Son Jesus to die on the cross for us. Jesus died for every thought, every wrongdoing past, present, and future. God is no longer angry with us because His full wrath was laid out on Jesus at Calvary. To claim and believe that God is still angry, would equate that Jesus died in vain. Every sin that we will ever commit was whipped on Jesus, nailed to the cross, and buried never to be resurrected. He still beckons us and calls us by name even when we wrong him time and time again!

Now that we are covered with the precious blood, when God sees you, He sees Jesus. In His word God says that Jesus is His Son in whom He is well pleased (Matthew 3:17). So if you are in Christ, then He is well pleased with you despite what you have done! Nothing can separate us from His love. He promises to never condemn us, and He forgets your wrongdoing. He makes promises to us they are true and valuable. God is not a man that He should lie, and it is not in His character to lead us in a way of deceit or condemnation. The problem is not with

His promises the problem is with us and how we chose to believe what is in His word.

Honestly, sisters, I struggle with this so much! I believe with all of my heart that Christ died on the cross for my sins and that He defeated death and then rose again with all power in His hands on the third day. I believe in that very truth, yet it is hard for me to believe that He is not upset with me when I do wrong or that because I did so badly in my flesh that He won't take care of me.

I believe in the truth that I will go to heaven when I die, yet I panic when my car note is due and my money doesn't look like it will cover it? For me, it is easier to believe in the promises that are yet to come, like heaven, than in the promises that can heal my current doubts and worries, like bills or relationships. Can you relate? Isn't that odd? It clearly says in His word that He will supply all of my needs according to His riches in glory (Philippians 4:19).

I have always struggled with trust issues, because for many years I was let down my people in my life. When I started college in Tennessee, they would always preach about viewing God as our Father. That concept alone was far too complex for me to grasp because, at the time, I did not have a relationship with my earthly father at all. So was I supposed to view the God of the universe as someone who didn't call to check on me? I did live with my dad for a couple of years when I was younger, and his priorities were always split between my sister and I, work, and his wife. I know that sounds like any other dad, but I constantly realized that me and my sister always ended up getting the short end of the stick. I believe because he wasn't around for the majority of my childhood once he got the chance, when I became a teenager, he didn't really know what to do. My mother was not around and my dad was physically present, but not emotionally there. I thought if this is how I am supposed to view God as a parent figure, then I don't really want Him.

God had to show me through Himself, and through others what reliable parents were supposed to look like. I can confidently say that every place that I have lived, I have a mother figure in that place! God is so faithful, because He also placed a physical father figure in my life too. (Sidenote: This past year, God started the restoration process with me and my earthly father)! When I lived in Tennessee, my campus pastors literally took me in. I recall one night that absolutely changed my life forever. I was really sad on the verge of hitting this solid wall of depression because it was close to the holidays, and I knew that my parents wouldn't call me. I would see my campus pastors just love on their kids, (They loved on me too) but I craved that from my own parents. I went into the living room where Chuck was watching his favorite football team on television, and when he saw that I had been crying he turned the game OFF, not down honey, but completely off and asked me what was wrong. We had talked for a while that night and he really helped me physically learn that's how God communicates with me too. When I talk to Him, He gives me His undivided attention, and He genuinely cares about what I am feeling! It took me a while to get to a place of being confident in His love for me, but I still fall short with the concept.

What I am learning, is to make every thought obedient to Christ. I am learning that when anxiety hits, to simply say *"God did not give me a spirit of fear but of peace love and a sound mind (2 Timothy 1:7)."* If you struggle with this too, we have to come to the realization that not all thoughts are from Christ. The enemy loves to try and change our thinking. If he can change the way that we think, he can change the way that we live. Have you ever met someone who had it made up in their mind that they just were not going to do a certain thing? No matter what you said, the evidence you brought, or how long it took you to lay out every fact, they just were not budging. That's how the enemy wants us to live. He wants us to become paralyzed to what God says is true! We have to trust the words of the Living God not a defeated enemy!

We tend to entertain the accusations and of the enemy instead of believing God. Let's say that you are a fast runner, and you know without a shadow of a doubt that your opponent is about to eat your dust when the gun pops for the race to begin. Now, given that information would you be at the starting line like *"I am just too afraid I know I am not going to win?" Maybe I should just go sit down and take the 'L'?"* No! You'd sound more like (If your level of sportsmanship is really little to nothing), *"This chick is trash (not literally), and she's about my eat dust for dinner!"*

Right?! Talk to the devil like the defeated enemy that he is!

Trusting has many different levels. You can trust that when you sit in a chair that it won't fall. You have faith in that chair. You can trust that your car will start when you put the key in the ignition. You have faith in your car's ability to work. Why can't you have that same trust and faith in the Almighty God that EVERY single word that He says is true? I recently saw a picture of two bodies of water that touch but they don't cross. How can we not believe in a God that commands water to go to a certain place but no further? He can command the world to stand still. He can change our situation in an instant. The issue is not in His ability the issue is with our lack of faith in His love for us.

If you love someone would you watch them starve while you had food easily accessible? If you love someone would you watch them walk in the rain while you sat in your car? Of course not! Sometimes, I feel that way towards God. I'll say you are sitting there with all power in your hands why won't you help me? I become increasingly frustrated when "my" time to fix the situation seems to escape, and the "deadline" to meet that very need seems to be sprinting towards me faster than a speeding bullet. Although I am being open and honest with God, I am also showing my lack of faith. Yes, I am proclaiming that He has the power to fix the situation, but on the other hand I am degrading His structure of time and sovereignty. A good friend of mine pointed out a very eye opening fact about God. He has framed us to function on the realm of time, but God Himself is timeless. He does not function on our barrier of time. He is sovereign. He sees all things and in Him all things function properly (Colossians 1:17). If we lived in a realm where time wasn't a factor, our lives would probably be a mess. I could not even imagine the dysfunction! God is bigger than time, He is bigger than deadlines and timetables. He sees all events about our lives from the very beginning to the very end. He knows when you will need a blessing and He knows when you will need a test to jolt your faith. He is all knowing!

I am not sure if any of you have ever experienced a parade before. As a bystander, we just see the next float coming. We don't know if we will like that float per say or if we will love it, but we know that the overall experience will be worth it, because well parades are quite enjoyable- to me anyways. Picture this, while watching the parade we notice that there has been a sudden stop in the flow. You are becoming quite agitated because you are waiting for the next float to come yet it is not coming. You feel as though you are missing out on all of the more enjoyable floats, and time is being wasted. . We as the bystander represent how we are now. We can only see what's right in front of us.

Now if we were to watch that parade from a helicopter then, we would not only know what would be coming up next, but we would be able to see the whole picture at once. That's how God sees our life. He does not only sees what is coming up next, but He sees our entire life from beginning to end. Back to our scenario, now because of God's aerial viewpoint, He sees that one of the floats has a flat tire, and if it were to continue towards you it would cause destruction to not only you but the others around you. So He commands for the flow to stop. He does not start the movement again until He knows that everything is totally fixed so that you are not harmed. That's our God. That's how he operates. He sees things in the natural and the spiritual that may never even be revealed to us. In this life there are situations and circumstances that have wounded us badly. God could have stopped it, but would you be who you are today without that hurt? Would your praise look the same? Would your harvest look the same? Will you trust Him today?

The second portion of our verse talks about the promise God gave to Noah. When I see a rainbow, I immediately think of that promise. He told Noah that He would never punish the earth again through a flood (Genesis 9:13-14). That rainbow is a symbol of God's promise. When I see a cross, I immediately think of God's promise for eternal life through Christ Jesus. I think that it would be helpful to use other symbols in our daily lives to represent Jesus. For example, when we see a bank, I immediately think of how much money I DON'T have. What if I changed my mindset to see a bank as a symbol of how my security isn't based on my funds, but my security is based on Christ?

When I see a gas station, I think about how without this fuel my car would be stranded. I'm going to revamp my mind to think of the gas station as the Holy Spirit and God's word. If you do not refuel ourselves with the King and what He says about your emotions and your very being, you will be stranded and without hope. Your lives cannot function when your spirit man is running on empty, just like your phone will not work if the battery is not charged.

Take some time over the next couple of days and make your own symbols to remind yourself of God's promises to you. Ask Him to guide you in the area where you lack trust and faith in Him. He is the peace giver and the Promise

Keeper. Trust in everything that He says about you. He is not angry with you. He loves you unconditionally.

#ThePromiseKeeper

### **Warriors are Clothed in Gems**

"Afflicted city, lashed by storms and not comforted, I will rebuild you with stones of turquoise, your foundations with lapis lazuli. I will make your battlements of rubies,

Your gates of sparkling jewels, and all your walls of precious stones.

Isaiah 54:11-12

"I have been getting attacked back to back to back to back. I become blessed with an opportunity just to have it taken away. Some of those setbacks have been a result of my actions, but some are just pure attacks from the enemy. It feels like I am stuck in dried mud up to my knees. The only time I can move forward is when it storms. Then the sun comes out, the mud is dried around my feet, and now I can't move forward all over again. I am tired of this cycle. I am weak. Lord, send the rains of blessings. How can I find strength in such a time like this? I want a season of sweat-less victories and not constant battles. I put walls around myself to keep from getting hurt. I feel like I am literally the strongest person I know. Most people don't have a clue of what I go through, but if they only knew what I go through on a daily basis just to make it through the day, they might end up reconsidering the way that they treat me.

—Hailey

Have you ever felt like the afflicted city? You know the city where after the tornado there's a hurricane, and then a flood, and then a drought? Nothing seems to be working. You feel as if you have been attacked by the enemy, time and time again. You fight because your life depends on it. You do all that you know to do. You read your word, you pray the scriptures over your life, and it still feels as if your prayers just bounce off every wall, and never reach the ears of heaven. You are tired and you are on the brink of giving up.

As I am writing this, I am currently on suspension from my job. It's always hard when you feel as though you're being punished for doing the right action. Or it seems that when you make a simple mistake, those that have done worse get a slap on the wrist, while you get punched in the face. This comes right after having my classes cancelled for school after my scholarship fell through. I worked really hard to get myself back into school after the heartbreaking situation at Tennessee. I feel as though every time I try and move forward with my education, that failure continues to haunt me. I just cannot catch a break. These moments do not compare to the times in my life when I have battled deep, black depths of depression due to rejection and abandonment issues. It's these very days where the depression seems to be creeping at my door. My city, which is my temple, my life, has been to war time and time and time again, and honestly I am tired of fighting.

I remember briefly telling you all earlier about my time spent in Montana doing a discipleship program with my summer job project team. My God, was that the hardest summer of my entire existence! When we all first met, I believe there were fifteen or sixteen of us in total, but we all had to share our testimony. I was so embarrassed of my story because it wasn't one that I was proud of. I had not yet come to the realization that my story was one of strength and not of failure. After my turn, I remember my Summer Job Project brothers and sisters continuously telling me how much of a warrior I was, and I kept hearing it from others even after I left Montana. Now I am five foot two and have never weighed more than ninety-five pounds in my whole lifetime, so being called a warrior was a little insane to me. Now, I have been called feisty before, but that's because I carry an attitude, and a snapback that can reach your great grandmother!

However, I later learned that this warrior people were speaking of, had nothing to do with my physical stature, and had everything to do with my spirit. I believe we all have a spiritual warrior within us, but sometimes our warrior becomes tired, and the armor becomes too heavy for you to carry. Some battles will be sweat less victories, and other times you may have the fight of your life, but remember with God, you will always be victorious (Romans 837; Psalms 108:13; Psalms 62:1).

The key is to never give up on yourself or on Him.

Perhaps, you have stopped praying or have stopped spending time with God, and now when the battle comes your warrior is not fully equipped or energized to complete the fight. Other moments, you have done all that you can and our Commander is putting total trust in you that you will fight with what you have learned. That doesn't always look like telling you the next steps, but trusting in His movements alone. That requires patience, faith, and complete trust. If you struggle with those in your walk, then the fight is going to be taxing on your spirit. We have to watch and listen for God to move, and sometimes that is difficult because we become so caught up in just wanting Him to give us the answers. Although Christ has won the ultimate fight, that does not leave us exempt from spiritual battles.

Get back to the foundation of victory because God promises to restore our broken city. The cities that are bashed by family, abandoned by mama and daddy, molested, raped, and thrown away, and tossed to wind by so called friends, He will restore them all. He will replace what we have lost. You have to train and strengthen your spirit warrior. Your armor may not fit snug right now. Keep praying and growing in knowledge and faith. Build your faith muscles and before you are aware of it your armor will be custom made just for you!

Watch and listen to where He is taking you, and be careful who you surround yourself with. When you are looking to be restored and revamped the people around you may be the ones hindering you from reaching your full potential in Christ. They can have draining spirits trying to attach themselves to you. Pray about every relationship in your life. Continuously ask God to add and/or remove people in your circle that are not on the path to your destiny, and when He answers, be obedient.

As women, we can have a strong will to be everything for everyone but ourselves. You want to be everything for that man, so you'll change who you are to please your god and not the God who created you. You'll want to be everything for that job, so you overwork yourself, and don't get enough rest which will result in you not to giving your best. You want to be everything for your family, so you push yourself to almost a breaking point. You're fighting for everyone, and there are people in your life who know that you will go above and beyond for them so they afflict your city with request after request. They know you will not say no, and that gives them an open door to use you over and over again. Here's a tip that I have learned and it has changed my ENTIRE life. Grasp and take hold of the spirit of **NO**. When you are overwhelmed and drained, you're not doing any good to anybody anyway. If God gave us His best, should we not give our best in all that we do? Just say **no** or **no thank you**, **not today**, **I am sorry but I can't**. It can be said in many different ways, but it all has the same meaning. I am not saying be rude about it and kick everybody to the curb. In some moments, just politely walk them across the street, and walk yourself right on back. That means leading them to a resource, because you're not their only resource or option. God will lead you when it comes to those who need to help. He will reveal secrets and motives to you, if you'll listen and obey. (Job 12:22).

When He moves, you move there also. When we do not hear God, we think that He has left us or given up on us. I believe this is not only a way to trust

Him, but to rest in Him. There's a story in the bible about Elijah. He had just come off of a spiritual high, setting the idols on fire. Right after that, Jezebel commanded that he be put to death. So Elijah got word of his death sentence, and he ran! Again, I am a holy paraphraser so bear with me, but you can find the elite version in 1 Kings 19. As he was fleeing, he decided to leave his servant in another town. When the storm is coming honey, don't drag everybody through the rain with you.

Elijah traveled all day, alone, and prayed that he could die. Have you ever been there just hoping to die? You're tired of running, and you have run out of options so you are begging to God to end it all. After pleading, Elijah rested, and as he was doing so God sent an angel to feed him and gave him precise instructions to gain his strength for the next step of the journey. Sister, the first step in the storm is to just rest. You can rest in knowing that He will give you the strength to get to the next step.

God knew Elijah was afraid when he received a death threat, and God knows that you are afraid too in your storm. In the passage of 1 Kings, God's solution for Elijah didn't come through the mighty windstorm, the earthquake, or the fire. God's answer Him was in the gentle whisper. Stop always looking for God to do a big production for answers that you need for your problems. Your answer may just be in the stillness of His voice. In the midst of a raging storm, when we are not comforted, all we need to do is simply rest in Him. He gives us this time to regain our strength in Him to move forward, and to put one foot in front of the other, so be more willing to be fully confident in the quiet responses.

Being suspended from work was clearly not in my plans, however there has been an overwhelming peace brought upon me. I have had time to rest in Him, and seek Him, and write. I believe that I had become so overwhelmed in the journey and the process that I left Him out. I wasn't praying unless I was in trouble, and I wasn't seeking unless I needed something fixed. God needed me to just slow down and regroup.

Before I began this chapter, I revealed to the Lord how tired I had become going through the same cycle. I shared my hurts and failures with Him. I became very transparent. He told me that He would heal me through my own words. Maybe there is something God has called you to do, and you have been putting it off, just like I have with finishing this book. Perhaps what He is calling you to do is where exactly where He will meet you!

As women, I know that we love accessories. We love any type of jewelry! Why? Because it is beautiful and shiny! Who wouldn't like that? I love how God incorporates beautiful stones to declare His promise to us. He knew what He was doing when He made us to fashionable in different ways, because He knew that we would understand the beauty in what He is expressing to us through this verse.

The scars we have carried and the storms we have endured or are enduring are not considered the end. He will restore. God says that he will build us with stones of turquoise. I believe that He wrote this and put the greatest jewels and stones on display to remind us our scars and our testimonies are what make us beautiful! He will make our foundations with sapphires. He will make our battlements of rubies.

Battlements are structures to castles, not only do they protect but they are recognized as breathtaking structures. When you see a castle, kings, queens, princesses, and princes enter your mind. We are royalty to God. Think about that, even with all that you've been through, you are royalty. You are a daughter the daughter of the King of Kings.

He will make our gates with sparkling jewels, and all of our walls of precious stones. The very walls that you have placed up in your life to protect ourselves are the very walls that the Lord will decorate to show the world that He is your protector, and they can become enticing to those around you to want to know more about Him. He can transform those walls of self-protection into walls of His sovereignty. He can turn the walls we have placed up to cover our insecurity in to walls of security. He can turn the walls we have placed up to feel protected into walls where His presence is alive and tangible.

I can't stress enough how important it is to keep going through this journey. I believe that God truly wants us to experience His best for us right here on earth not only in heaven alone. Some Christians settle for mediocrity in this life, because they think that is all that God has for them until they reach heaven. Not so!

I believe that the scars that we have acquired on our way to glory are signs of strength and beauty and not of weakness. They are signs that our inner warrior has not given up. It shows others that if my warrior can make it through this then your warrior can too. Jesus did not escape earth without taking scars with Him to heaven. He is proud of them. They represent the ultimate victory! Your testimony is nothing to be ashamed of. God chose you to live this life because you are strong enough to live it. He entrusted you to make it through with His help. He is proud of you. He is proud of our inner warriors. Don't lose hope. Keep pressing, and keep listening to the Commander's voice. I encourage you to continue to put on your full armor and fight.

#YourScarsAreJewels

## Peace Brings Purpose

All of your sons will be taught by the Lord, and great will be your children's peace. In righteousness you will be established: Tyranny will be far from you; you will have nothing to fear. Terror will be far removed; it will not come near you.

Isaiah 54:13-14

"I strive to be great. I strive to be a leader that someone people can look up to. I want to lead other women into God's healing power. But first, I have to experience His power for myself. I want to know Him more than anything. It is my heart's desire to know Him fully. Yet sometimes I fear that when I pray for certain things, that he will allow me to be attacked by them. Is that a part of the Christian walk? Is that a part of learning who He is? I don't want to have cowardly prayers. I want to be strong in Him and confident in Him above all else."

—Isabella

        I have truly enjoyed allowing you all to be a part of this book and opening up the pages into the real time of my life. I may or may not know who you are personally reading this book, but I am glad that you are here. I just read my devotional for today in my *"Jesus Calling"* book. It is October 7, 2015, and today's passage was on releasing our worries and our fears to Him and entrusting Him regarding everything that concerns us. Sometimes, that is hard to do when life feels like it's swallowing you whole.

        I am still suspended from work so my biggest worry right now would be my employment status. How can we trust God when we do not see what He is doing? The answer is faith. Faith is like a muscle. When we want to gain muscle we must continuously work out. You can't just lift weights one time and expect hulk like muscles. You have to keep going back to the gym, even when you're sore. You have to go back even when you're tired. Eventually, you will begin to see the fruits of your labor. Faith is the same way we must continuously work out our faith in order for it to become stronger. You have to continue to trust Him even when it's dark and there seems to be no solution in sight. When it becomes stronger we have the ability to carry more without strain. I have shared with you how small I am, and if you have seen me in real life you are well aware that I am no bigger than a second. If I were to try and lift 200 pounds right now at the gym, it would be an epic fail!

I remember one year in high school, I believe I was a sophomore. I was living in Washington state at the time, and one of the requirements was to take a weight lifting class to graduate. Ugh, the struggle was all the way real. I remember my teacher saying that we would have to lift in front of the whole class one day, but he didn't make me lift as much as everyone else, which I was very grateful for. So I had to at least bench press the bar with no weights on it to get a decent grade. Now, mind you, I went in there, honey just as confident as could be. The class was gathered around just waiting to see what would happen. Thank God that phones weren't as prevalent as they are now. I would be all over the internet. Honey, memes and all! Anyway, the spotter was in place, and he let down the bar. Now, nobody or their mama's informed me that this bar itself was 45 pounds which was five pounds more than half my body weight!! When the spotter let go of the bar, the bar went sideways and so did I! Now, if I had been working out and lifting more, lifting that bar would be a piece of cake.

Imagine having just enough faith to carry the small things in life. We can miss the bigger opportunities to be used by God, and to see God in everything. He doesn't place us in situations that will harm us, and we do not ever have to be afraid. He is our Heavenly Spotter, so if we start falling sideways, He will be there to get us on the right track. Fear and tyranny will not crush us.

Like Isabella, we can have a lack of faith when we pray about certain situations because we fear that God will make us do something that we do not want to do. Let me be very clear on this God is a good Father. He knows what is best for us. Not everyone will be called to serve in Africa so just calm down if that is your fear. Not everyone is called or equipped to teach the children so if you have some kind of toddler phobia, I am sure He is not going to call you to go teach children's church. God has equipped us with our very own special and unique gifts. He will equip us to walk in those specific gifts, not the gifts he has given our fellow brothers and sisters. If it's in what God has called you to do, sometimes, there will be moments where you won't want to do what He's told you. Will you trust your emotions or will you trust God?

The scripture says that all of your sons or children will be taught by the Lord. I believe that means, for all our mothers, your children that you have birthed or adopted, and like we discussed in our first chapter, our spiritual children will be taught by the Lord. He uses us to be vessels for His kingdom. If we were all called to execute the same gifts then there would be many children unreached.

The Lord says great will be your children's peace. I don't have any children of my own just yet, but I have heard that when a pregnant woman is stressed, the baby can feel that stress to because the child is connected to the mother. The spiritual children we are called to teach are looking at directly at us, they are attached to our peace. My Bishop constantly tells us, our lives may be the only bible others will ever read. Those who are attached to our obedience are connected to the Life

Support within us, just as a fetus gets nutrients from an umbilical cord. They are attached to our Peace, our Strength, our Life, which is Jesus.

When you go to work and constantly have a negative attitude, but proclaim you're a Christian, the others around you will not be attracted to the God in you. If you consistently gossip about others, but with the same tongue say that you love Jesus, others will not want to open their lives up to you. If you sleep around, but stress to those around you how important it is to attend church on Sundays and live for God, do you think they'll want to join you? Why would they? Why would they need to answer to a God they cannot see when their god sleeps right next to them? What are you showing to the world? What makes your peace different then their tainted view of the peace they have now? If we only show them negative view points, like walking in our own ways, instead of walking with the Lord, we will lead them astray.

Some of you will pray for God to place you in the greatest of positions. There's nothing wrong with that. However, in the beginning, your intentions may have been valid, but when God answered your prayer you aborted or abandoned the mission. Don't be obedient to God until HE answers your prayers and places you in a position of royalty, and then leave the harvest to fend for themselves!

Some leaders in the church have purposely led others astray because of the power and status they hold within the church. They have become selfish and lovers of selves. They have thrived and thirsted after people worshipping their praise instead of worshipping the living God. Let us not become that. God entrusts us with the lives He has given us to nurture. His word says that tyranny (the misuse of power) will be far from us. (2 Timothy 3:2-5). God will allow it to be removed from us, but let us remember not to actively invite it into our lives. Study the bible for yourself. Make sure that the leadership that you are under, wholeheartedly preaches from scripture to lead the flock, not just from social media to gain likes and followers!

Social media has become such a phenomenon in our generation and cultural. Be mindful of what you post for others to see and why you are posting it. Social media can be the greatest ministry platform, but it can also be the greatest distraction. Whatever you post, allow it to be uplifting and not let it steer your brothers and sisters in the wrong direction. Your accounts can be your biggest stage, and people are watching. Be wise.

When I said that God entrusts us with lives, I am sure I scared a few people with that statement, but remember we have nothing to fear. If God is for us who then can be against us (Psalms 118:6; Romans 8:31)? That verse applies to you too. At times, you could be in your own way. Sit down and rest. Let Him lead. His word says that terror or fear will be far removed from us, and it will not come near us. If we are not connected to Him, He is more than able to recruit others to help His people to safety. Or God could just do it all by HIMSELF! He loves His people whether we chose to be a part of His plan or not! When we chose not to seek God regarding His will, and do not do what He tells us to do, someone else will replace us. (Esther 4:14). He has strategically chosen us for a certain time to help a certain kind of people.

Don't believe the lie that you are too old or too young to make a stand for Christ (I Timothy 4:12). People are constantly watching your witness whether at work, on social media, at school, even your family at home. They are watching your life, and they want to know how to live for Jesus whether they ask you personally or not. When we are truly living for Christ, His peace coincides with our spirit, and He is with us. When we chose to walk in His peace and His light we walk fearlessly in our purpose, so do not fear. His peace that carries all understanding will give you the strength to carry out what He has called you to do.

#HavingHisPeaceBirthsPurpose

### *A Friend Who's a Hero*

"If anyone attacks you, it will not be my doing; whoever attacks you will surrender to you. See, it is I who have created the blacksmith who fans the coals into flame and forges a weapon fit for its work. And it is I who have created the destroyer to work havoc;"

Isaiah 54:15-16

"I have never had real girlfriends before. Something always happens where they think that I am better than them or that I just think too highly of myself. Then the rumors start and then people tend to have a tainted view of who I really am. Whenever I am put in a new atmosphere, whether it be a new school or a new job, after people find out how goofy I am, they always tell me when they first met me they thought I was stuck up. It never fails I lose friends because people either think that I am jealous of them or that I am too good for them. I have my own problems and issues and I just wish I had true friends to share them with."

-Lyla

Friendships are truly important in this walk of faith that we are on. Some of you may have been blessed to have had friendships for many years and some of you may not be able to say that we have been blessed with human relationships, and that's okay. I want to share something that God shared with me one day. One particular night, God had told me to stop hanging with a group of people who I thought were my friends. One person in that group had been my best friend for a while, so I was really grieving the fact that the Lord was telling me to stop being friends with them.

So I prayed, and I prayed long and hard too. I prayed just as Gideon had prayed when He needed confirmation from God. Gideon had asked God to show him an answer by laying a cloth on the ground and asking God to make the cloth wet with dew and the ground surrounding it dry. There's some holy paraphrasing going on right about now, but God did that for him. Then, just to be sure, He asked God to make the cloth dry and the ground surrounding it wet. God did that too (Judges 6:36-39).

So that night, I asked God for a Gideon experience of my own. God agreed. After I had fallen asleep, I had this weird dream, and when I woke up I thought well that was odd. The dream didn't make sense to me at first so I just kept going about my daily routine. I had an event to go to that day in my small hometown, and I was brushing my teeth, the Lord broke down the very dream that I had labeled weird just a few minutes earlier. Every person from the group of friends that I was told to distance myself from had a part in that dream. It was my very own Gideon experience.

However, I wanted to be extra sure like Gideon, and God continued to reveal their true hearts towards me. I began to wallow in self-pity about how nobody liked me…blah blah blah! I know a few of you have been there as well. Then the Lord said this to me: "I have placed you in a position like no other. Some people are so wrapped up in their earthly relationships that they will never experience me on the level that you will."

That shook me to my core and self-pity no longer existed in my heart, because God thought so much of me to take me on winding roads, through this life's journey, all so I could be closer to Him. In that moment, not having parents around or a group of friends didn't even matter. Since then, God has placed a few loyal people in my corner that I know I can go to for prayer or advice. I felt He decided that even with the promise that was given that human relationships were still necessary. He is still guiding me on when to let others go because some relationships started with great potential, and then ended up falling short.

The people who have hurt us and let us down, God created those people, and quite frankly He loves them just as much as He loves us. It can become easy to blame God for everyone else's actions, but God has given every person the power to make their own decisions. Do you realize that animals and plants and the stars don't have that same power? That's why he says that *"If anyone attacks you it will not be my doing."* People won't always make the best decisions regarding your hearts and feelings, and if you're truly honest, you haven't made the best decisions on behalf of others either. God doesn't want you to sit stagnant and victimized for the rest of your life. What good will does that do? The enemy would love to have you stuck forever. When you live your life as the constant victim, you will never experience the freedom of being the victor.

God wants us to walk in freedom. If you can't find true friends, still be friendly to others. Ask God to send you trustworthy people, but in the meantime, find your friendship and comfort in Him. He is the only one who will not disappoint you, and if that is truly your heart's desire God will supply you with friends who not only love you, but they also love Him. It's a beautiful thing. God will reimburse you for your hurts. It may not be in the way that you think it should be, but it will be beneficial. I used to think that when others hurt me, their punishment should be to get hurt worse than I did. I was rushing in my mind to reimburse them for all that they had done. I was trying to play god, because He declares that vengeance is His alone (Romans 12:19). Let Him fight for you. Rest, sister.

I have come to learn to hear God's voice, and I have been blessed to constantly experience a level of discernment that allows God to keep me from harm, if I will be obedient. There are some people that I know that will just not like me, but I try to love them anyway. If Jesus is the light and you are His child, you carry the Light within you. Sometimes, your very presence will shine a light on a dark situation within a person. Their disdain for your presence has nothing to do with you, but has everything to do with the presence of God within you.

God has shown me schemes and plans that people will try to plant against me and others around me, and the whole time He is constantly protecting us. Guess what, He is protecting you too, whether, you see it or not. I have learned to fight back with prayer and not with pettiness. Like, I will legit tell on you to God if you come for my life! That to me should scare someone more than gossiping about me to your girlfriends.

There comes a level maturation when you realize that some of the friends or a job that you have lost without warning or explanation is God's sovereign protection over you. They were probably scheming to take you right out, and instead of God allowing you to be put in a position to mend the relationship, He cut it off at the root! When we secure ourselves in Him, no matter what anybody does to us or what anybody says to us, their actions will not overtake us.

I encourage you to not give into your immediate emotion of anger and the feeling of betrayal when you read that God has created the destroyer to wreak havoc. Think of it like this, Jesus is our very own superhero. A good superhero cannot show how powerful He is without a villain right? How lame would Batman be without the Joker? Jesus bled and died so that we, too, can be victorious over the enemy and his schemes. People keep talking about how awful our world is becoming, but Jesus is returning. A superhero doesn't come to the rescue in a time of peace. He is still pursuing us with His powerful hand. He is mighty. He is strong, and He is in love with you, and He is mighty to save!

My all-time favorite verse in the entire bible is Romans 8:37- *"For overwhelming victory is ours through Christ Jesus."* Have you ever been overwhelmed before? Usually when we think of being overwhelmed it is associated with something negative, but God has a habit of turning negatives into positives (Romans 8:28). He turned death into life, and judgment into grace and mercy. He is turning every battle in your life into overwhelming victories. God cares about every aspect of your life, whether it be big or small from your viewpoint. If friendships or relationships are important to you, He will take care of it. Sometimes, the process starts with you, alone. If you want better friendships, be a better friend. When you set appointments to meet with someone, be courteous enough to be on time, or let someone know if you cannot make it. Be kind, just as you would want someone to be kind to you. What you want to receive is who you ought to become.

#WhatAFriendWeHaveInJesus

## The Declaration

"No weapon formed against you will prevail (shall prosper) and you will refute every tongue that accuses you; this is the heritage of the servants of the Lord, and this is their vindication from me, declares the Lord."

Isaiah 54:17

"I had a dream. There was a grand couple's ball. They all met in a gorgeous ball room before they proceeded to the main venue. The walls were polished gold with pictures of angels painted on the ceilings. The floor was the shiniest I had ever seen in my life! There were tall, thick gold-floor to ceiling columns in sections of the room. Me and a couple from my church came in late from working overtime on the week's service. We were in our street clothes while everyone else had on their most glamorous gowns and the finest tailored suits. I went to the back to help the woman I was with get ready, and due to her being ready to pop with a baby any day now, she wasn't able to bend in certain places to put on her dress or shoes. I kept apologizing for making them late, but her kind spirit kept reminding me our lateness was for the greater good of getting the youth prepared for that upcoming week.

After getting her all dolled up we went to meet her husband. When we found him, they told me they felt awful for leaving me. I told them not to worry and to have a great time that night. I sat down in one of the many red plush chairs with gold trimming watching all of the couples take pictures, laugh, and love on one another before departing to the main venue. I noticed my mother and her husband, but of course she didn't acknowledge me. I felt the all too familiar sting of rejection. Then, the director gathered everyone's attention and had the men line up on the left side of the ballroom and the women line up on the right. They were to walk the long runway and meet their significant other front and center so everyone could see them. Music came on and the first male and female began on the long walk to meet their love in the end. Once they met, the man held his arm out for his woman to link her arm into his signifying their union and then they would disappear down the long hallway leading to an undisclosed exit. I watched every couple with a broken heart because I wasn't in a pretty dress meeting my love at end of the grand ballroom. Then I recognized a single guy from my church and thought maybe he'd playfully walk with me just to fill the void once everyone had gone, but I soon realized he was there to escort his sister. My dream had once again diminished. So here I am, in street clothes watching the so called elite with their lovers walk to a grander venue to enjoy the evening. Once the last couple had gone, the director turns her nose up at me, directs the music to be silenced, and turns on her heels and walks down the long hallway to direct the rest of the evening. As I sit in silence, rejection, and sorrow for a few minutes, I begin to hear harps and trumpets and beautiful angelic voices. It was such a holy sound, but not too overwhelming. The room became that much brighter and I look around to see guards standing at attention for the coming of the King. I look to the left and there is the King of Glory in a white robe walking down the long pathway to meet his love at the end. Me! He gives me a gentle look, a nod saying head to the right, and then a glorious smile. There I was in my street clothes walking to my first love, the King of Kings himself! The funny thing was I felt no shame with what I had on. I felt like a princess in my sweatshirt and jeans. He lifted His arm so that we could connect. We didn't leave that place as the others had. We just danced and danced and danced. I never felt so loved in all of my life. Jesus reminded me there that even in my worst state, in a grand place, I too, was worthy of love."

—Leilani

For the short time that I was in school, in my theatre class we had a brief discussion about heritage. Heritage is defined as something that is passed down as a tradition or inherited by birth. Some cultures practice the same rituals for hundreds and hundreds of years hoping to accomplish a desired end. That end could consist of joy, pride, and/or honor. Jesus declares that nothing will prosper against us that is our heritage according to His word. When you became a Christian, you were born into God's family. The traditions for His children, now includes you! Your desired end is Jesus Himself, and the promise of His is vindication for you.

I loathe hearing people throw this verse around out of context. No weapon formed against me shall prosper, so I can sleep with my boyfriend and not get pregnant. No weapon formed against me shall prosper, so I can slander my husband with my words and have him respect me. No ma'am that is not how that works. You can't just pray and seek when you're in turmoil. You can't just praise to get a breakthrough. You may have become so accustomed to singing and shouting, but does heart and lifestyle look any different? You know the scriptures, but are you living them out? We rebuke weapons and declare that they won't form, but are you inviting them into your life?

I believe that this is God's declaration to us that even after we have been through war and high waters, nothing else shall harm us again. Nothing else shall tear down our spirits. Nothing else shall call us unworthy or unloved. Nothing else shall overtake us ever again.

God declares that this is the heritage for the servants of the Lord. To be a servant means to give your life for your master. It means to be fully devoted to His plan, His will, AND His timing. I know that timing concept can be the hardest pill to swallow, yet we must remember that God does not set us in places too early or too late. No matter how impatient our flesh tends to be, He always brings what we need at the appropriate time. (Psalm 145: 14-21)

No weapon, No words, No man, No job, No DEVIL can prevail against us, because we are His, and He will fight for us! Our refuting days are long gone. The definition of refute is to prove someone wrong. We, as women, love to prove somebody wrong, honey! That arguing spirit is on some of us heavy! No longer are you going to have to explain yourself. God is your vindicator, no matter what sister so-and so has to say about you! We will silence every tongue that comes against us.

Sometimes, it is truly hard to declare over our lives what God has already declared over us. I believe that in order to prevail and keep going we have to do just that. Honestly, I struggle speaking His promises over my life. I allow the circumstances to blur my faith's vision. However, it only takes that one leap or that one word to get me going. Sometimes I stutter when I start off, and sometimes I am even nervous, but I do it. Start declaring God's word. Even if we have placed ourselves in the situation that we are in through our words or actions, God still declares that this is His vindication for us. This is our way out through Him.

In order to declare the Word, we must KNOW the word. Many Christians are in battles that are overtaking them because they do not know the Word of God. Everything that we will ever need is that book. The bible has become so easily accessible now through technology that there is no excuse to not read it. We, as Christians, have become lazy in our faith. If someone spoon fed us the word, many of us would find an excuse to not eat it! Remember whatever you need is found in His presence. What weapon you need is found in spending time with Him. It is in His presence that you will find healing. It is in His presence that you will find hope. It is in His presence that you will find peace and acceptance.

I have to share a secret with you, ladies. When I started writing this book for us, I wanted to share my story, but I didn't know, through my own strategies, how to do it in way that wouldn't be overwhelming. Each short testimony or story in the beginning of each chapter is MY story. The beginning letters of each young ladies name at the start of each chapter spell out:

I have dealt with depression like no other, and each time it resurfaces it comes with a new face. I shared how I tried committing suicide with Elizabeth's story. Which is actually my middle name, but honestly that wasn't the first time. I am from a very small town in north Georgia, and one year I was making my way home for thanksgiving from Atlanta. I had been in the midst of quite a few storms at that time. My uncle who I was close to had recently passed from cancer on my mother's side. This was a year after my cousin passed and I wasn't able to attend location purposes. I still regret not going. Those two events were a hail storms within themselves.

I wanted my uncle to be free from pain, but I also, selfishly, wanted him to stay. The doctors had given him about three days to live, and he held on for two weeks! I remember one of the last times I went to visit him in the hospice and he looked at me and said, *"Girl, don't cry. I am about to go to heaven. You should be happy!"* It was a few days after that conversation that I finally felt at peace, and he passed two days later.

I was stressed from the passing of my uncle. I was stressed from seeing a mother that had not been present and because it was her brother who passed, knew she and her husband would be present at the funeral. I was stressed because I was in a season where I was dating this guy, and I really loved him. I almost thought he was the one, until he called, and I heard a woman's voice in the background. He hung up on me, and didn't call me for three days! In between those days with no communication was my uncle's funeral! I was stressed from the drama at work. That was just a monsoon of heaviness all by itself!!

After all of that, on my way to thanksgiving I totaled the first car I have ever had!

I was taken to the doctor the next day because I didn't feel the impact of the accident until then, because adrenaline can be very numbing to the body. The doctor gave me these muscle relaxers and instructed me to only take half of one, once a day, due to their strength. I knew at that time with everything going on at work (this contains a personal story of another person, so I will not go into detail) however, I knew that I probably wasn't going to last much longer there.

At that time, I began cutting again as well. It was coping mechanism I picked up in high school when I didn't feel loved by others. I thought about how no one loved me. I thought about how I just wasted three years on a guy for him to just not talk to me. This was a habit of his, but I never thought that it was someone else in the picture. I just wanted to love and be loved so much that I accepted his behavior. I thought about how if my mom and dad loved me that they would talk to me more like other people's parents did. How I was always reminded that my cousins were better, and that they deserved more love at family gatherings. I thought about how I was always forgotten or overlooked. I honestly still struggle with that last thought till this day. I thought about how if I was good enough my life wouldn't be so dark and difficult. So I took every pill. I didn't sleep for three days! God told me in the middle of one of those sleepless nights that if He allowed me to fall asleep, I would not wake up. I was mad at Him because that was the whole point! I didn't want to be alive. I didn't want to wake up! I didn't want to feel the pain and heaviness anymore! I remember crying out to Him and pleading, "Lord please just let me go."

Instead of answering my prayers, He took me on a journey. It was like having an outer body experience. He took me to the times in Tennessee when I had to quit school in Tennessee, and work from five in the morning until one in the morning of the next day. He showed me how He was with me and had angels assigned to me in those times when I would start walking at 5 am to get to work by six, and again when I got off at midnight and wouldn't get home until 1 am. I lived near a mental hospital, and it wasn't the best of neighborhoods, but He protected me. I vividly remember a man one night that was sitting on the steps and he said to me, "Young girls like you should not be walking in the dark alone." I instantly got chills and became very afraid, but he never got up off of that step. I never understood why He didn't move until that night God showed me what looked like two glowing angels one standing on either side of me!

He showed me the nights on my air mattress when I would just cry because I was so tired and depressed. He said to me "Look, there I am right next to you. I know every hurt. I know every tear. I know every pain. I have always been there, and I am here with you now."

After that experience I remember feeling at peace. Life didn't automatically work itself out after that night either. Life's circumstances didn't just change in the blink of an eye. I lost my job that following January, and I moved four times within that following year. Life hit me hard, but I made it. I made it to share my story with you. I made it by changing my perspective. I made it by changing my attitude. I made it by make a choice to trust instead of fear. This journey didn't happen overnight, and there are many times that I have fallen over and over again, and God is there to pick me up. He is there to remind me that I am still His no matter what I do, what have do, and what I will do! He is that crazy faithful. Nothing I do surprises Him, but His love in spite of it all, always takes my breath away.

I hope that my honesty has inspired you to not be ashamed of your story.

I hope that this book has given you a reason to not give up. On this journey, I have wanted to quit more times than I have written about, but I couldn't. The enemy has fought me over speaking to you all because he wants us to be stuck. Today no matter, what I am going through, no matter what the day looks like, or even what yesterday looked like, I am choosing to be unstuck in Jesus name. I am choosing to take one more step. I am choosing to read one more verse. I am choosing to pray one more prayer in Jesus name. I believe that for you and for me that that one more step will be the step that puts us in motion, and that it will jumpstart God's purpose and will within us all. I love you all so much, and I am truly believing with you that God is sovereign over our past and all of its hurts and that we will proclaim the love that God has poured out through us in Isaiah 54. I declare that we are women of God that He has called and created us to be (Jeremiah 29:11), and that nothing in this life or the next will stop His love from reaching down and embracing us (Ephesians 3:18). I declare overwhelming victory is ours through Jesus Christ our Lord. (Romans 8:37) I declare that we are a royal priesthood (I Peter 2:9). I declare that we are the apple of His eye. I declare that His love for us supersedes our greatest fears and our deepest wounds. I declare that we will see signs and wonders in this generation. I decree and declare that the sleeping warrior within us is awakened, by His stripes we are whole and healed, and we are strong because WE ARE HIS!

#YouAreAWarrior

Loving you,

*Chelsea Elizabeth*

## *Dedication*

I dedicate this book to the Love of my life.

Abba,

I haven't always been faithful. I haven't always been obedient. I haven't always loved, and yet through it all You have been the strength of my existence. You have kept me afloat throughout the many times that I wanted to give up on this journey called life. You have healed me. You have restored my heart, which I deemed irreparable. You changed it from lumps of dust to a heart of flesh. You have held me above water. You have wiped my tears. You have forgiven my sins past, present, and future. You have given me hope. You are the best Mother, Father, Friend, and Lover that I have ever known. I could not have my next breath without Your presence. You are my everything, and my words, my life, could never be enough to express my gratitude for this life YOU have equipped me to walk through. Thank you for holding my hand, and cleaning my scars. Thank you for placing the right people in my life at the right time. I dedicate this to You because you gave me this dream and vision, and helped me carry it out. You trusted me enough to walk through the fire and to help others along the way. Thank you for hearing my prayers, and most of all Thank You for just being who You are: The Great I AM. I love You, Lord♭

<u>*Thank You*</u>

Teresa (Vic) Beasley

Cristal Connelly-Diakate

Andree (Kerry) Cox

Tam Crockett

Ruth (Andrew) Guerrier

Scarlett Habersham

Chrystal Hill-Hawkins

Wanda Hill-Hawkins

Shekia Hill

Toravia Hill

Debra (Douglas) Johnson

Laurie (Chuck) Lester

Nikki (Harry) Parker

Quemeka (Jonathan) Rivera

Thank you to every mother (and their spouses) that have children of their own, yet thought and loved me enough to include me in their families! The spectrum falls between whether giving me a place to stay when I was in need to just giving me a hug, wiping my tears, and giving me advice. Thank you for being the light, and giving me hope that there are people who display genuine compassion and love. I appreciate you dearly, and I love you beyond life. I pray that God blesses you beyond measure for thinking to love His child as if I were your own.

Thank you to Jason Serrano for helping me with this book. Bro, I could not have done this without you! Thanks for taking time to help me and give me advice on this journey.

To my little one in heaven,

I hope I am making you proud. I hope that you were happy when you were with me for that short period of time. I can't wait to meet you. Thank you for giving me a newfound strength, and most importantly a newfound love of life. Some days, I still cry because I think about you often, and wonder how life would have been different with you here. I love you forever and always.

Lastly,

To my beautiful sisters, Quemeka, Toravia, and Shekia. I love you guys to the moon and beyond. We have been through so much yet we are smarter, more beautiful, and stronger because of it. Y'all mean the absolute world to me, and I cannot thank y'all enough for being the most amazing big sisters that anyone could ask for. We are great! We made it! We are victorious no matter what anyone says about us.

I LOVE y'all!

(Hill girls forever, even when we all get married) HaHa!

www.ingramcontent.com/pod-product-compliance
Lightning Source LLC
Chambersburg PA
CBHW071128090426
**42736CB00012B/2059**